The Social Conscience

of the Evangelical

The Social Conscience
of the Evangelical

Sherwood Eliot Wirt

HARPER & ROW, PUBLISHERS

NEW YORK, EVANSTON, AND LONDON

Grateful acknowledgment is made for permission to use the following quotations: lines from *The Complete Poems of Robert Service*, reprinted by permission of Dodd, Mead & Company (New York), The Ryerson Press (Toronto), Ernest Benn Ltd. (London); lines from "The Everlasting Mercy," by John Masefield, © 1912 The Macmillan Company, renewed 1940 by John Masefield; lines from *Pansies*, by D. H. Lawrence, Martin Secker Ltd., by permission of Viking Press (New York), Laurence Pollinger Ltd. (London), and the estate of Mrs. Frieda Lawrence; quotations from *Restoration Puritanism*, by H. G. Plum, © 1943, The University of North Carolina Press; from *Situation Ethics*, by Joseph Fletcher, © 1966 by W. L. Jenkins, used by permission of Westminster Press (Philadelphia) and SCM Press (London); lines from "The Anguish," in *Collected Poems*, Harper & Row (New York), © 1928 by Edna St. Vincent Millay, renewed 1955 by Norma Millay Ellis, by permission of Norma Millay Ellis; and from *Creed or Chaos*, by Dorothy L. Sayers, © 1947, used by permission of A. Watkins, Inc. (New York).

FIRST EDITION

LIBRARY OF CONGRESS CATALOG CARD NUMBER: 68-11736

A-S

TO THE MEN OF THE TEAM

"In whom high God hath breathed a secret thing. . . ."
—*The Coming of Arthur*

Foreword

For a long time I have been waiting to read this book—or one like it. My friend and colleague, Sherwood Wirt, has given us an exciting evangelical perspective on social responsibility, and he has done it with candor, with courage, and with grace.

The Social Conscience of the Evangelical is significant not only for its content. It is notable because the writer is not a social "expert," but a busy editor associated with a movement of aggressive personal evangelism. He is setting his social concern right in the middle of his evangelistic zeal. Let those who criticize evangelists for a social "blind spot" take note!

As I read the manuscript, I felt two mingled reactions.

There was gratitude for what was being said and how well the author was saying it. Dr. Wirt's book is clear-eyed and perceptive. He knows his eternal faith. He is also aware of the world in which he—and we—are called to live this faith. His approach is modest and balanced. He indulges in no blanket denunciations of the past or present church. Nor does he make "overclaims" for the influence of the Christian in society.

I also felt remorse. It is to the shame of the evangelical church that Dr. Wirt pinpoints our failure of social responsibility over the last century. This is a denial of our Bible, our history, our belief—indeed, of our Lord. This book illuminates the reasons for evangelical backwardness in the social arena, but does not excuse them.

Dr. Wirt has dealt keenly with the major issues of our decade. He has not given a detailed blueprint for an evangelical social thrust. His approach is provocative, not exhaustive.

Is the "needle" of love not precisely what we need most? Our insistent demand for the "how" may mask a fear to become really involved. Commitment to Christ must involve commitment to our neighbor and our world, for Christ's sake. Evangelism must sound this note today with the conviction of the classic evangelical tradition.

When I had finished *The Social Conscience of the Evangelical* I thought: "I wish I had written that!" I pray that God will use this book to help all of us to live it!

—LEIGHTON FORD

Charlotte, North Carolina
August 1967

Preface

One June day in 1965 the author was privileged to spend several hours in Chicago with a group of Christian leaders. Among them were Dr. Ted W. Engstrom, Dr. James Forrester, Dr. Frank E. Gaebelein, Dr. Lars Granberg, Dr. Richard C. Halverson, Dr. David A. Hubbard, Dr. Harold J. Ockenga, Rev. Floyd W. Thatcher, and Dr. Curtis Vaughan. A consensus reached at that meeting was that a study of the evangelical social conscience was long overdue.

The present work could be called an indirect result of that gathering. It owes much to the inspiration of these men, together with others, but should not be taken as a necessary reflection of their views individually or collectively. A host of teachers, colleagues, classmates, and friends have contributed unconsciously to the preparation of the volume. Some are given due credit, many are not. Where quotations have not been traced to their proper source, amends will be made in future editions as notice is received.

The scope of the discussion makes it difficult for a journalist to claim technical competence throughout. Nevertheless a sincere effort has been made to subject the material to scholarly scrutiny. Where errors of fact have crept in, or where the evangelical Biblical position has been inaccurately presented, the book stands ready to receive correction.

Several chapters were presented in the form of lecture series to students and faculties of three institutions: Bethel Theological Seminary, Minnesota (1966); Fuller Theological Seminary, California (1967); and Sterling College, Kansas (student retreat, 1966). They were also shared with the Minnesota ministerium of the Evangelical Covenant Church (1966). Nearly all of the book has been offered over a period of months on four midwestern radio stations: KTIS, Minneapolis, Minnesota; KNWC, Sioux Falls, South Dakota; KFNW, Fargo, North Dakota; and KNWS, Waterloo, Iowa.

The author would acknowledge special assistance received from friends who have read most or all of the work in manuscript: Dr. Carl F. H. Henry, Dr. Horace L. Fenton, Jr., Dr. Ockenga, Dr. G. Aiken Taylor, and Mrs. Lois Weigand, the latter being associate editor of *Decision* magazine. Their many suggestions have been helpful and, indeed, indispensable, as have the editorial contributions of the Religious Books Department of Harper & Row. Mr. Carl Moen of the Minnesota State Conservation Department kindly reviewed Chapter 11.

The writing of SCOTE (as the manuscript came to be called in the *Decision* office) took place amid the active tasks of editing a magazine and serving on the Billy Graham Team. That the project survived at all is due to a wonderful staff. Miss Ethel Beckstrom, editorial assistant, prepared both the original and the final typescript, and voluntarily spent hours of her own checking references. Without her skillful help and signal devotion to duty, it is doubtful that the book could have been completed. Mrs. Ruth McKinney, my secretary, has cared for the considerable correspondence involved. Miss Charlene Anderson has efficiently handled the securing of many permissions. Mr. Robert P. Blewett, Miss Alice Sundstrom, and Mrs. Becky Dodson have given counsel and encouragement. My beloved author-wife, Winola Wells

Wirt, has as always been unfailing in support.

A substantial portion of the royalties of the book have been designated, in appreciation, to the ministry of The Billy Graham Evangelistic Association.

Acknowledgments are due to the staffs of the University of Minnesota library; the Minneapolis Public Library; the libraries of Bethel College and Seminary, Luther Theological Seminary, and the United Theological Seminary, all of the Twin Cities; and to the University of Chicago Library and the Evangelical Library of London, England, for many courtesies rendered. The librarian of the Graham Association, Mrs. Mildred Weasler, has gone the second mile in providing books and references for a baffled researcher.

Finally, the author wishes to extend appreciation to Dr. Billy Graham for the contribution he has made to the sensitizing of the evangelical social conscience. Dr. Graham is an evangelist for Jesus Christ, to the glory of God; but as the *Humanitas* student club at Columbia University has pointed out, he is also a great friend of the human race.

—S. E. W.

Minneapolis, Minnesota

Contents

Foreword by Leighton Ford vii

Preface ix

CHAPTER 1. Introduction to a Conscience 1

CHAPTER 2. Where the Action Is 6

CHAPTER 3. Humanity in Galilean Homespun 19

CHAPTER 4. Voices out of the Long Night 27

CHAPTER 5. The Human Factor 37

CHAPTER 6. Plumb Bob on the Saints 47

CHAPTER 7. The Call and the Calling 55

CHAPTER 8. Interlocking Freedom 65

CHAPTER 9. God Made a Colorful World 79

CHAPTER 10. Right Versus Wrong 91

CHAPTER 11. The Defilement of the Earth 102

CHAPTER 12. Blessed Are the Peacemakers 113

CHAPTER 13. Making a Stab at the Issues 129

  Church and State—Poverty—Highway Safety—Capital Punishment—Abortion—Euthanasia—Unnatural Sex—Alcohol—Tobacco

CHAPTER 14. The Horse and the Cart 147

Notes 157

Selected Bibliography 169

Index 173

Chapter 1

Introduction to a Conscience

This book it chalketh out before thine eyes
The man that seeks the everlasting prize;
It shows you whence he comes, whither he goes;
What he leaves undone, also what he does . . .
This book will make a traveler of thee . . .
Yea, it will make the slothful active be.

—John Bunyan,
Prologue to *The Pilgrim's Progress*

Convinced it is the will of God for her life, a Berkeley coed joins a student protest demonstration.

At the end of a trail of bitterness and frustration, an alcoholic war hero encounters Jesus Christ. He devotes his life to changing tough young delinquents into Christian citizens, with the backing of his state government.

The Illinois Christian college that produced three of the five Auca missionary martyrs of 1956 uses the same student zeal to operate a rehabilitation center in Chicago's inner city.

A Christian literacy team, on safari deep in the Congo, devotes weeks to the task of teaching primitive Africans to read and write. To the tribespeople the members of the team say, "We learned this from Jesus."

An aristocratic Ecuadorean *patrona* who ruled her river land with an iron will decides, after attending an evangelistic

1

meeting, to devote her efforts to giving the poverty-stricken river Indians a better way of life.

A converted British food merchant hears the Gospel and opens a halfway house where recently released prisoners can live in good surroundings until they are fully rehabilitated into society.

Members of a Christian student club at the University of Washington conduct weekend tutorials in remedial instruction for underprivileged minority children in Seattle's Georgetown.

A former wiretapper for the crime syndicate, now a Christian, joins with New York City police to provide educational opportunities for worthy young Puerto Ricans in Spanish Harlem.

These examples suggest a changing sentiment in the evangelical Christian community of our generation. A sense of social responsibility, buried too long, perhaps, under the wrong kind of conservative instincts, is rising to the surface and demanding a place in the sun. People who accept the authority of the Bible are beginning to outgrow a limited approach to the basic social problems of twentieth-century living.

This development is part of the new life that is flooding through the whole evangelical movement. Thousands of young people in the West are discovering that man was made to enjoy God, and that to be a Christian is the most exciting thing in the world. They look upon what James Hastings Nichols called "the evangelical undertow"[1] as the wave of the future. The feeling is not restricted to the grass roots. The whole of Christendom was surprised by the vitality demonstrated when 1,100 delegates gathered at the World Congress on Evangelism in Berlin late in 1966. Christian leaders such as Frank C. Laubach, Carl F. H. Henry, Billy Graham, Paul Smith, Corrie ten Boom, Kyung Chik Han,

Oral Roberts, Chandu Ray, Bob Pierce, and others moved historic evangelicalism into a new dimension. The recent interest shown by the World Council of Churches and its related organizations in "conservative evangelicals" is a reflection of the fresh confidence that is breathing through many evangelical groups—a renewed sense, it might be said, of dependence upon the Spirit of God.

The typical Gospel church of our day is not the fundamentalist enclave it was at the turn of the century. Its congregation still wants its minister to be fervent, dedicated, evangelistic, and Biblically oriented, but a new element has entered the picture. Today's evangelical congregation wishes its pastor also to be imaginatively and effectively cognizant of the social ferment going on about him. It does not want him taking political sides, but it wants him socially sensitive to all sides. It wants his prayers to reflect the truth that God is in the world as well as in the church. It wants his sermons to give out equipment for dealing with the "space age" in the mode of the living Christ. Some evangelical seminaries have forged ahead of the congregations in the matter. Without forsaking the spiritual heritage of the faith, without reducing the content of the Bible, they are implanting in their men and women students the conviction that the Christian, because he is a member of the human race, has inescapable responsibilities to society.

The new deep tide of conviction running through the old churches has many sources. The congregations have been exposed (sometimes in spite of themselves) to the environment of the atomic age, the new concern for survival, the shifting theological winds. They are sensing in a new way that they have a stake in the human race, that all people are bound up together in the bundle of life; and that before a man can, by the Grace of God, be "called out" (which is the meaning of the Greek word for "church"), he first has to be a part of that from which he is called. Dr. Emil Brunner explained it: "Before one can become an evangelist, he must first be a human being."[2]

It needs to be set out at the start, then, that members of evangelical churches are finding out as perhaps never before that they are flesh-and-blood people. There is nothing unbiblical about this view. Christians are told in the Bible that they are one with men everywhere; that the same God who brought the Israelites out of Egypt also brought the Philistines from Caphtor and the Syrians from Kir.[3] The Christian shares his mortal tent with Jew and Greek, barbarian and Scythian, Oriental and Ethiopian, Roman Trappist and Jehovah's Witness; with Reorganized Mormon and Black Muslim. Yes, and with atheist and agnostic, with beatnik and deviate, with addict and arsonist and Viet Cong guerrilla. But also with the good, gentle folk of earth wherever they are to be found.

In seeking to express this kinship evangelicals prefer to avoid the doctrinaire use of the expression "brotherhood of man." They have felt it is not realistic. Historically the church has consistently held to the brotherly potential of man; the Word of God does not set a limit to what the Holy Spirit can do in establishing brotherliness among men. But today's evangelical, as the author has attempted to understand him, is as pragmatic as his contemporaries; he looks for a brotherhood that works. He sees Ananias going to meet a Gestapo-type religious fanatic named Saul of Tarsus and calling him "Brother Saul."[4] He likes that. But idealistic optimism, whether bourgeois or Marxist, he eschews in favor of the facts of human nature. He says with Masefield,

> We're neither saints nor Philip Sidneys,
> But mortal men with mortal kidneys.[5]

Another burden today's believer would like to deposit somewhere is the quarrelsome history of the past. He disclaims interest in scooping up the acid flung about in old theological wars and pouring it into new bottles. Neither is he concerned to push everyone into some particular camp or other. He recognizes one major battle, with the devil, and in that struggle he knows, as the Apostle said, "The weapons of our warfare are not carnal."[6] That there have been vital turning points in Christian history, he would be the last to deny. The evangelical is not about to scuttle the Protestant Reformation; a piece of his soul belongs to the sixteenth century. But his heart and his head and his feet are in the late twentieth, and he knows it is today that his witness will be made, if it is made.

There is a sense in which it does not matter what the court of human opinion thinks of the evangelical. His ultimate responsibility is to his Lord, and it is before his Lord that he will be judged. There is another sense, however, in which the whole evangelical movement is being placed under judgment by the social sciences. Does the Good News really produce, as is maintained, persons of ultimate worth? Are the changed lives of believers exhibiting the kind of social concern that was so characteristic of Jesus?

The pages that follow are an attempt to explore the works that, according to the New Testament, invariably follow true faith. The past is prologue to the present. Our concern will be the direction the evangelical's social conscience is taking at this moment of history. There is no doubt that Jesus Christ left chart and compass pointing a course for his followers. Some today are already on their way. Many are eager and impatient to get started. But to those evangelicals who still wonder why they have to go anywhere, a personal word may be permitted: it is because, brethren, *we can't stay here!*

Chapter 2

Where the Action Is

*Of what purpose is the multitude of your sacrifices to
me? says the Lord. . . . Bring no more vain offerings to me. . . .
Wash yourselves, make yourselves clean . . . cease to do
evil; learn to do good; seek justice. . . .*

—Isaiah 1:11-17 (Peshitta)

In some of the exciting new translations of the Epistle of
James, Christians are challenged to become well-rounded,
fully developed, whole personalities for the carrying out of
God's commission among men. Evangelicals who seek to
emulate their New Testament forebears in the faith can aim
therefore at being the most ecumenical persons on earth.
They have a flying start, for matters of protocol and tradition
are of decreasing concern to them. A worship service may be
as free and informal as a testimony meeting, or as traditional
as the order of the *Book of Common Prayer,* and it will suit
them. If the evangelical does not like the form of worship in
which he is brought up, he has the option to find one that he
does like. This spiritual freedom always operates, of course,
within the *sine qua non,* the love of Jesus Christ, and it is
to the credit of many evangelicals of past and present that
they have recognized that love wherever they found it.

With improved communication between churches, today's
man of faith is outgrowing the temptation to turn his de-

nominational haven into some kind of holy fort. Internecine warfare between believers who do not baptize, worship, or tithe in an identical mode is subsiding. Is Jesus Christ enthroned in a brother's heart? Does he measure his life by the God-inspired Scriptures of the Old and New Testaments? Except in unusual circumstances the evangelical of the sixties and seventies will not insist on pressing the agreement farther. He is committed to the view that the tie that binds is not ecclesiastical union, or uniformity of worship, or doctrinal niceness, but rather fellowship in the Beloved.

There is a lyrical retroaction to such ecumenicity, for it lays claim to the rich, full heritage of historic Christianity. As the Apostle Paul wrote to the early believers, "All [things] are yours; and you are Christ's; and Christ is God's."[1] It means that the testimony of the early martyr Perpetua, the memoirs of the immortal Augustine, the superb preaching of Chrysostom, and the singing heart of Francis of Assisi all belong to the evangelical, together with the zeal of Luther, the brilliance of Zwingli, the warmth of Wesley, and the genius of Rembrandt. In the arts a special kind of thaw is taking place, so that today's evangelical community in increasing numbers is enjoying (for example) the Gregorian chant, Palestrina, and the Bach chorale along with the Gospel song.

The new translations also reveal in a fresh way that the Apostle James had a highly sensitized social conscience. "Now what use is it, my brothers, for a man to say he 'has faith' if his actions do not correspond with it? Could that sort of faith save anyone's soul? If a fellow man or woman has no clothes to wear and nothing to eat, and one of you say, 'Good luck to you,'. . . what on earth is the good of that?"[2] James has many provocative things to say about Christians putting into practice the message they have received from Jesus. He makes explicit what is implicit all through the New Testament: that the Christian social conscience should be as wide as the love of God in Christ. It belongs on the same plane as his ecumenical sense of fellowship in the Gospel, for that fellowship is founded on an evangelistic outreach to all men. Jesus Christ preached to the multitudes, he had compassion on the multitudes, he died for the multitudes. As he was in the world, so also are we.

Thus the historic social concern of the church belongs to today's Christian along with the prayers, the noble thoughts, the great statements of belief, the literary and artistic treasures of the church down the centuries. When a man becomes a believer he does not retreat from his responsibilities as a member of society; quite the opposite. He takes his place in the tradition of Moses, Amos, Hosea, Isaiah, Micah, Jeremiah, Mary, James, and John the Baptist.

It is the lasting glory of the Hebrew people that they produced so many centuries ago the first known champions of social justice. Men and women of every race and nation around the world recognize today the contribution of the prophets of Israel to the ordering of human affairs. It is not surprising that the American plantation slaves seized upon Moses, standing before the Egyptian Pharaoh and crying out, "Let my people go!"[3] as their spokesman nearly three thousand years after his day. Moses is the hero of oppressed peoples. He is the liberator who leads the victimized populace out of bondage and into a normal place in the family of mankind. The prophet Amos, in turn, was the prototype of every protesting minority as he stormed into Bethel crying out, "Let justice roll down like waters, and righteousness like an ever-flowing stream."[4] Justice! Not charity, not compassion, not the largesse of a generous potentate, but the rights of a man clothed with dignity because he was made in the image of the Creator and made for God. Here is the divine plumb line applied, under the Spirit of God, by a shepherd from Tekoa to such widely scattered issues as race, poverty, war, real estate profiteering, and discrimination against minorities. Each of the Hebrew prophets in turn made a surgical analysis of social conditions and rendered his verdict.

" 'What do you mean by crushing my people, by grinding the face of the poor?' says the Lord God of hosts."[5]

"There is no faithfulness or kindness, and no knowledge of God in the land; there is swearing, lying, killing, stealing, and committing adultery; they break all bounds and murder follows murder."[6]

"The godly man has perished from the earth, and there is none upright among men; they all lie in wait for blood, and each hunts his brother with a net."[7]

"Thus says the Lord: Do justice and righteousness, and deliver from the hand of the oppressor him who has been robbed. And do no wrong or violence to the alien, the fatherless, and the widow, nor shed innocent blood."[8]

" 'Yet you say, "The way of the Lord is not just." Hear now, O house of Israel: Is my way not just? Is it not your ways that are not just? . . . . For I have no pleasure in the death of anyone, says the Lord God; so turn, and live.' "[9]

Churches whose orientation is toward the Bible are learning that a serious study of the social context of God's revelation is a rich mine of spiritual teaching. They are becoming acquainted with the world to which they are called to carry the Gospel. Such studies indicate that there is no special orbit in which God's man is supposed to move, apart from the main stream of life. The Christian is expected to become *involved*. If the prophet was not a political lobbyist, neither was he a hermit. If our Lord Jesus Christ was not Barabbas, stirring up rebellion against Rome, neither was he Simeon Stylites, living out his life atop a pillar. The early Hebrews learned at the foot of Mount Sinai that in the sight of God there is indeed a difference between the sacred and the profane, but there is no difference between the spiritual and the social. Social wrongs, to God, are moral wrongs. So the Mosaic code became a body of law unique in the ancient world, and if some of its legislation looks primitive to us, in the ancient Mediterranean world it was a Magna Carta. Divinely promulgated as the basis of a nationalistic society, it aimed to be fair even to the stranger within the gates.

Through the institution of the Year of Jubilees the Hebrews were able to raise up a bulwark against the social evils of economic oppression and slavery.[10] All the societies of the Mediterranean were slave societies. In recent years historians and anthropologists have unearthed evidences of the attitudes that past cultures took toward slaves and captives. Slavery developed out of military conquest. The pyramids of Egypt are monuments not so much to a royal dynasty as to an ingenious, cruel system of keeping captives busy. The Book of Exodus corroborates the Egyptian records of slavery as it was practiced by the Pharaohs. The Roman Republic developed a whole corpus of law for the regulation of slavery. In Sparta there was systematic terrorizing of slaves. Primitive tribes around the world considered the slave to be utterly without dignity or rights. For millions upon millions of enslaved people in past centuries, and even down to the present day in outlying pockets of civilization, survival has been a matter of supreme indifference because of their condition of bondage. The warrior who preferred death to capture was not necessarily being brave or noble; he was being realistic. Even in sophisticated Athens and Rome, where household slaves received humane treatment and were accorded special privileges, their lives were never out of jeopardy. Four hundred slaves belonging to the Roman Pedanius Secundus were ordered put to death because they were under their master's roof when he was murdered.[11]

In Israel a different note was struck. The deadly cynicism and contempt for human life that underlay ancient society was challenged by men who thundered, "Thus saith the

Lord!" A basic element in modern life found its beginnings in the Hebrew word *mishpat* (justice). A man's life, it seemed, held worth. The intent of God's law was to throw arms of protection around the less-favored members of society. The laws of the Pentateuch "are not the laws of a society which has no problems"; far from it. "But they are laws and they are the laws of a society which is really concerned with the establishment of human community."[12]

The Old Testament's social position has been well summarized by Canon Stanley Evans: (1) the service of God is ethical before it is ceremonial [but not before it is loving and believing]; (2) God is concerned with corporate morality; (3) a first moral duty is the demand of justice for the poor; (4) the purpose of God is national perfection; (5) there will be no national perfection—there will not even be national survival—while the people forsake the ways of God.[13] Out of such ore has been milled the Christian social conscience. Even after thousands of years the church finds it difficult to improve upon the words of the 146th Psalm:

Happy is he that hath the God of Jacob for his help,
Whose hope is in the Lord his God;
Which made heaven, and earth, the sea, and all that therein is:
Which keepeth truth for ever:
Which executeth judgment for the oppressed:
Which giveth food to the hungry,
The Lord looseth the prisoners:
The Lord openeth the eyes of the blind:
The Lord raiseth them that are bowed down:
The Lord loveth the righteous:
The Lord preserveth the strangers;
He relieveth the fatherless and widow:
But the way of the wicked he turneth upside down.[14]

Does the New Testament manifest a social passion to match that of the Old Testament? The question has usually been debated on the basis of prior commitments, with more heat than light. Conditions in the Roman Empire in the first century A.D. were different from those in Palestine in 600 and 700 B.C., when the prophets were speaking. However, it may be said that the New Testament's social outlook shows a dominating concern for the welfare of men. A generous, friendly, humanitarian interest in people breathes from every page from Matthew to Revelation. God's will is sought and obeyed because it is in the best interests of men. The heart of the Good News is that "God so loved the world."[15] The New Testament, like the Old, is grimly aware that forces exist to hold back the human race and to prevent its full flowering under God. Among them are poverty (Luke 6:20); war (James 3:1); discrimination (Colossians 3:11); superstition (Galatians 4:9); immorality (1 Thessalonians 4:3); slavery (Revelation 18:11-13); and oppression (Mark 10:42-43).

One of the most inspiring documents of Scripture is the Magnificat of Mary, found in Luke 1:46-55. Although it is chanted in churches daily around the world, Mary's poetry is not always clearly understood. "The meaning of this revolutionary song is obscured by our clinging to an English past tense for it which does not really express the prophetic Hebrew."[16] For Mary is singing, as Dean Spence says, "as though the future had become the past."[17] Her Magnificat is pealing out the victory of God over humanity's traditional enemies:

He has scattered the proud in the imagination of their hearts,
He has put down the mighty from their thrones, and exalted
    those of low degree;
He has filled the hungry with good things, and the rich he has
    sent empty away.[18]

The Magnificat has been called a battle hymn of democracy, and it is no accident that the words should come from the lips of a Galilean peasant girl who was to give birth to the Messiah of Israel. The text shows a refinement of some powerful ideas expressed in the ancient Song of Hannah as recorded in 1 Samuel 2. It speaks of the maiden's exultation at the tremendous honor that God has bestowed on her, but it also betrays a boldness that makes Mary seem almost like an Israeli *sabra* (youth) of today. This young girl was apparently voicing the same kind of rebellious patriotic fervor that erupted ten years later in the revolt of Judas of Galilee. During that revolt Mary was the mother of a growing family, and perhaps she watched from the nearby hills while Caius, acting for Publius Quintilius Varus, the Roman general, burned the neighboring Galilean village of Sepphoris in reprisal for its support of Judas.[19] Hundreds were crucified and thousands enslaved in that episode of horror. Galileans had a lot to remember, and Mary was a Galilean and a Zealot.

> He has helped his servant Israel,
>> In remembrance of his mercy,
> As he spoke to our fathers,
>> To Abraham and to his posterity for ever.[20]

Mary was also a prophetess who knew that the Lord God was on the verge of doing great things. The "system" must go. The redeemer and deliverer of Israel was knocking at the door of history. Let the sons of Herod tremble. Let the keepers of empire beware. God was about to undo the work of power-hungry men and to give the earth back to his people. He would somehow liquidate the arrogant military and economic oppressors. In the light of that manifesto, let us look again at the words of Jesus, spoken to his mother some thirty years later at Cana: "O woman, what have you to do with me? My hour is not yet come."[21] It may have been that Mary's target date for revolution was out of line with her Son's eternal purpose for mankind. Whatever the proper exegesis, the time is overdue for a fresh appraisal of Mary's social conscience.

Of the other voices speaking out of the New Testament to the social problems of the day, two are from Mary's family. One was John the Baptist, who as a youth undoubtedly came under the influence of his older cousin. John is an enigmatic, ascetic figure over whom scholars have puzzled for two thousand years. The recent Qumran discoveries have not helped decipher the mystery as much as was hoped, for there seem to be no links between the Dead Sea community and John's social message. Could the clue to John be Mary? As his statements are recorded in the New Testament, John preached the universality of man, the voluntary distribution of wealth, and the sharing of surplus food. He demanded repentance and high ethical standards, and denounced corruption in government. John was an authentic prophet in the Hebrew tradition, even to his prediction of the Messiah to come.

One statement of John needs attention because it has been misinterpreted for centuries. When some Roman troops sought advice after one of his preaching missions, John said (in the words of the King James Bible), "Be content with your wages."[22] Most readers of that passage since A.D. 1611 have probably assumed that John was counseling economic quietism—"I suggest you do not press for a wage increase at this time." John meant nothing of the kind. What did he know about military wage scales? He was urging the soldiers to stop bullying and extorting from the citizenry of Palestine. Let the troops live within their incomes and stop milking the countryside.

The other voice in Mary's family was James, the Lord's brother, whose position on social matters has already been noted. James, too, has sometimes been misunderstood; his invective against exploitation has been interpreted to mean that he opposed the Gospel of salvation by Grace through faith. Yet all James sought to do was illustrate the Gospel's full meaning by showing the relationship of works to faith, and deeds to words. The New Testament would be unthinkable without his balance.

Luke the physician is another New Testament writer who may have sat under Mary; how else could he have known what she "pondered . . . in her heart"?[23] Luke alone records the Magnificat; and the spirit of that song pervaded everything he wrote that has come down to us. Renan once called Luke's Gospel "the most beautiful book in the world," mainly because of the social compassion that breathes through it. As the first historian of the early Christian community, Luke described the experiences of the disciples in the social maelstrom of the first century. He recorded the attempts at communal living that were outgrown as the teaching spread and new churches were gathered. Crisis after crisis was survived, and in each case Luke pointed out the underlying social and economic factors.

The Apostle Paul is sometimes accused of being a social quietist; yet his letters were penned to grapple with a variety of community issues: political exploitation, military service, racial and religious intolerance, the consumption of food used in pagan ceremonies, the position of women, propriety of dress, relations with non-Christians, taxation, prostitution and pederasty, control of disease, relief of poverty, and the handling of civil jurisprudence. All these issues were dealt with according to the principles of Scripture, the witness of the Spirit, and the best information available to meet the conditions of the day.

Such a taste of social insight and criticism leaves us hungry for more. Why did not someone strike out, for example, against the slave traffic? By New Testament times it had reached far worse proportions than when the Old Testament was being composed. Two-thirds of the populations of the great cities of the Mediterranean were in bondage. Gibbon estimated that there were sixty million slaves in the Roman Empire.[24] Once a twentieth-century Holy Land tourist has wandered among the gigantic ruins of Baalbek and Jerash, and has seen at first hand the kind of toil to which a first-century slave was consigned for life, he finds himself asking questions. How could an intelligent Christian disciple, reduced to dragging one of Nero's ships across the isthmus of Corinth, fail to leave behind some kind of social protest? Or finding himself spending the best years of his life hauling a single stone block from a quarry to a pagan temple, how could he have failed to speak of the judgment of God upon such evil?

At this point opinions differ. The Reformation Anabaptists of the sixteenth century declared that the church, as a spiritual body, should have nothing to do with the *magister*—that is, with the powers of government. Some Mennonite and other Protestant groups still hold this view. Certain Reformed churches participate actively today in the duties of citizenship, but believe that their sense of concern for society does not justify their making ethical demands upon governments that do not acknowledge the primacy of the name of Jesus Christ. They say that while John the Baptist may have rebuked the pagan Herod Antipas for his immorality (Matthew 14:4), John's example was not representative of the New Testament. Still other evangelicals see in Jesus' famous quotation from Isaiah 61 a direct assault on the institution of slavery.[25] Further, they believe that our Lord's command to proclaim the *kerygma* before kings and governments (Mark 13:9) does involve a moral demand and an ethical imperative, whether the magistrates be Christian or not (Acts 26:18). Why then was there no protest against slavery by the early Christian church?

Under Roman law there were two classes of men: freemen and slaves.[26] To escape from the curse of lifelong bondage, three avenues were open. One was manumission, which was unlikely and unpredictable at best. Another was the resort to flight, which meant spending one's remaining days covering up one's brand, hiding, living in continual dread of capture, torture, and death. The third was armed and bloody insurrection against the might of the legions. Rebellion meant cruel and inexorable retaliation; in the case of the rebellion under Spartacus, men were nailed to crosses from the Tiber all the way to Brundisium. Rome, the mistress of *Mare Nostrum,* was not about to change her social ways for anyone.

To explain the attitude of people in New Testament times toward slavery, it might help to look at analogous conditions in mainland China today. Why have not Christian disciples behind the Bamboo Curtain (and we know there are some) spoken out since 1950 against the evils of Marxist socialism? Why have they not openly condemned the regimentation, the invasion of family life, the dehumanization, the brainwashing, the persecution, the hate mystique? The answer is obvious: for most people such a protest would be unthinkable. A few have tried it, with pathetic results.[27] Is it not the "People's Government"? (And was not Rome known as the *Senatus Populusque Romanus*—S.P.Q.R.?) Some day (so the Christians of China believe) God will act in his sovereignty. Meanwhile there is a cross to carry.

Anyone who reads the New Testament imaginatively, of course, can soon sense its attitude toward slavery. The trafficking in human lives is esteemed on about a level with impure water, highway robbery, and leprosy. Slavery is the kind of evil which, if a man can, let him by all means avoid (1 Corinthians 7:21). The New Testament looks beyond to a day when the distinctions between slave and freeman will be gone forever.[28] The Gospels show us not only man as he is, but man as God intended him to be. Butterfield rightly says, "I have never been quite convinced . . . that the Christian Church was responsible for the emancipation of slaves in the Roman Empire. But I am utterly convinced and a thousand times more impressed by the original teaching of Christianity—namely, that in Christ a man was free, actually felt himself exultantly free, and could be conscious of reaching the profoundest depths in life, even though he was a slave. On this view we can say that Christianity flourishes independent of regimes and political orders—it may capture any regime—and I have yet to be convinced that political regimes can ever really destroy it."[29]

The teaching of Christ did actually begin the social ferment which upgraded slavery to serfdom, and eventually opened up the conditions under which men of courage and faith could force the establishment of a free society. Ernst Troeltsch writes in *The Social Teaching of the Christian Churches*, "As soon as a message of this kind creates a permanent community a social order will inevitably arise out of this program. . . . The command to love one another . . . is bound to influence [the] community [and] lead it to make an attempt to realize this idea in practical life."[30] Not simply slavery, but every social issue of the ancient world was to be affected by the Gospel of the Kingdom of God as proclaimed by Jesus Christ. The results, however, were not always as beneficent as Professor Troeltsch suggests. It is the unspeakable tragedy of the church that where it spread the Gospel, long-suffering humanity soon found itself in many ways worse off than before. How such a development could emerge out of the greatest message that was ever given to men is something hard to explain. Perhaps in the pages that follow some intimations may appear.

Chapter 3

Humanity in Galilean Homespun

*I tell you, in so far as you did it to one of the humblest
of these brothers of mine, you did it to me.*

—Matthew 25:40 (Goodspeed)

Jesus of Nazareth appears in the Gospels as the exponent of
authentic, normative human behavior, of the kind of life that
God intends every man to have. It is a life of freedom, of
dignity, of joy, of fellowship, of fulfillment, of victory over
temptation. In his own case the social context varied from
adulation to crucifixion, yet his bearing was consistent
throughout. According to the promises of Scripture, God
has made this kind of life available to every man through
faith in Christ. For every man has a right to be restored to
his true nature and to live as a forgiven child of God; every
man has a right to be saved.

"I came," said Jesus, "that [you might] have life, and [that
you might] have it more abundantly."[1] "If any one thirst,
let him come to me and drink."[2] Today men are still endeavoring to plumb the depths of those words. In the urban-
ized West, life has become unbelievably different from what
it was when our Lord walked through the hill country of
Palestine. While squalor and hunger persist in our midst,
affluent societies offer unprecedented comforts and pleasures;

19

automation is bringing leisure to rich and poor alike; medical wonders are reducing the ravages of invalidism and pain; on every front the borders of human knowledge are being pushed back. To speak theologically, God's gifts to men appear to be limitless.

Yet the Christian believes that the greatest blessing of all comes not so much from what a life contains as from the life itself. He looks upon the whole drive and thrust of what he calls the "life in Christ" as supernatural. He links its motivation to the Holy Spirit and its rationale to the sovereignty of God. Thus day after day, in good times and bad times, in Mediterranean villa or Watts slum, in gentle zephyr or icy williwaw, the believer finds himself sustained and encouraged by the good hand of his Maker. The "abundant life" he accepts as neither an achievement nor a possession but as a free gift. He does not measure it by progress charts; he does not evaluate it with time and motion studies. The miracle of Jesus Christ, as he sees it, provides men with a new dimension of living. Christian people over the centuries have used many words to try to describe that dimension; they have spoken of salvation and forgiveness and reconciliation and eternal life and many other concepts. Yet there comes a point at which abstract nouns fail to communicate and other media must take over. So some believers call up images of a Hound of Heaven, or a rainbow in the sky, or a leap into the unknown, or a great divide, or a washing away, or a cross in the heart. They know that all such images are inadequate to describe what has taken place, yet they feel and hope that some impression may be conveyed of what is bursting to be made known.

Before one can appraise the social conscience of the evangelical, he must try, at least, to appreciate what makes an evangelical. It has very little to do with what is called the "conservative instinct" or the "fundamentalist mentality," but it has everything to do with Jesus Christ. The heart of evangelical belief is the conviction that when Jesus of Nazareth laid down his life outside the walls of the Holy City, he introduced a change into the moral structure of the universe. Thus the confessing believer honors the "cross of Calvary," not because of the beauty of the tradition that surrounds it, not because of the symmetry of its shape or the texture of its wood, not even because of the red blood that streamed down it. He honors the cross because of the man who hung there and bled to death for the sins of the whole world. This was the Lord Jesus Christ, whom the Bible calls the bearer of men's griefs, the interposer for their transgressions. Evangelicals believe that Christ was crucified not only *by* the whole human family, but *for* the whole human family. "He was wounded for our transgressions, he was bruised for our iniquities: the chastisement of our peace was upon him, and with his stripes we are healed."[3] Scripture says that out of love he did it; there was no other way.

Dietrich Bonhoeffer will be best remembered for his description of Jesus Christ as "the man for others."[4] In the view of the whole Christian world, the title fits. Everything about Jesus, from his miraculous birth through the radiant Galilean ministry to the shocking events of Passion Week, is seen in Christian eyes as attesting to the unselfish design of his life. He lived and died "for others," that is, "for us." To the evangelical it means that Jesus Christ was God communicating with men to give them back what they once had, but which they had lost through sin: fellowship and communion with the unseen Creator.

When a man who has reached a point of faith seeks to relate his personal life to the social environment in which he moves, he soon finds himself over his depth. It is not that he is beyond help; it is simply that becoming "spiritual" has not eliminated his problems. His gifts, his disposition, and various aspects of his character remain about what they were. However, there are now resources available for dealing with the issues that keep cropping up, and if he has the will to make use of the help, he learns that the power that saves can also keep. The resources can best be described by referring to John 16. In this passage Jesus told his followers, "It is a good thing for you that I should go away. For if I did not go away, the divine helper would not come to you. But if I go, then I will send him to you."5 The divine helper is, of course, the Paraclete, or the Holy Spirit. Jesus was predicting for his disciples an imparting of spiritual power such as they had never dreamed of. He was pointing ahead to Pentecost and to the prospect of victorious Christian living to take the place of the haphazard confusion they had known.

But in his role as the Messiah and the Savior of men, did Jesus Christ also provide a working basis for participation in the social order? That is the question with which our study is concerned. Did the Founder of Christianity lay a foundation for the modern Christian's social conscience? It will not do to quote isolated texts or reaffirm the old clichés. There are large-scale questions of motivation and purpose that need examining. Differences of environment must be bridged. The Christian requires to know whether he can authentically take a stand for social justice in the twentieth century *in the name of Jesus,* in the full sense of that expression.

The sociologist of religion referred to earlier, Professor Ernst Troeltsch, gave his opinion that "the message of Jesus is not a program of social reform," but is on the contrary "obviously purely religious in nature."6 Troeltsch sliced the distinction so finely that he seemed to permit Jesus no interest at all in the social lot of mankind. Yet many times in the Gospels our Lord is found using expressions that indicated he knew of no dichotomy between the "religious" and the "social." Whether his social views reflected the influence of Mary, his Galilean mother, is worth speculating about; but there is no doubt that Jesus recognized his affinity to John the Baptist and the prophets of ancient Israel, and to their social messages.

The Gospels represent Jesus at times as a champion of the economically dispossessed. We see him exalting love for neighbor along with love for God. He reaches out to foreigners who are beyond the borders of the "Israel of God." He seeks the release of captives, prisoners, and slaves. He denounces the scribes and religious leaders who "devour the houses of widows."[7] Despite his well-known requirement of loyalty that surpasses family ties, he insists that a man put the care of his own parents ahead of his obligations to his religion.[8] His treatment of women is radically opposed to the strictures of that day. He exhibits sympathy and understanding toward children. He operates an out-patient clinic wherever he happens to be. He insists upon justice as the basis for everyday dealings between citizens. The social teaching of parables like "the Good Samaritan" and incidents such as the encounter with the rich young ruler have had an effect upon his followers that cannot easily be measured. If one summary statement of Jesus' ethics can be made, it is that love of God is best shown by love of fellow man.

In general, then, it can be said that Jesus evaluated an individual's spiritual life in terms not of religious exercises, but of ethical and social derivatives. "Not every one who says to me, 'Lord, Lord!' shall enter the kingdom of heaven," he said, "but he who does the will of my Father who is in heaven."[9] The evangelical Christian would say that the very fact that Jesus consciously laid down his life for others provides a dimension of infinity in his view of human relationships. "Greater love has no man," he said, "than this, that a man lay down his life for his friends. You are my friends. . . ."[10] Jesus consistently lifted the worth of human life above the minimum levels to which the ancient world had reduced it. "Of how much more value," he said, "is a man than a sheep!"[11] He asserted that men were worth saving, that the individual member of society had inestimable value in God's sight. But he was not content with a humanistic approach; he espoused a principle of spiritual freedom that would release men for even greater service to humanity, and he died to give it eternal significance. In the Parable of the Last Judgment, Jesus emphasized in the strongest possible terms the importance of such social work as the feeding of the undernourished, the care of the sick, the rehabilitation of prisoners, the clothing of the destitute, and the housing of refugees. According to Matthew 25:40, he interpreted the activity of his disciples in any one of these areas as being the same as devotion to himself as Lord.

Yet it must be added that our Lord's primary interest was not the shoring up of a sagging social structure, but the ushering in of an altogether new order. He was the proclaimer of the Kingdom of God, and that imminent event could not help but affect his attitude toward some of the social issues of the day. Thus he disposed of Herod Antipas, the vacillating tetrarch of Galilee, with a cryptic, "That fox!"[12] When asked to render a verdict on an inheritance dispute, he demanded, "Who made me a judge or divider over you?"[13] Questions of taxation and divorce he answered seemingly with reserve, as if unwilling to be drawn deeply into the issues involved. Jesus never for a moment believed that his Kingdom would be rung in simply by an improvement in the external conditions of human life.

The new social order heralded by the Messiah was intimately connected with his own small group of disciples, and with the people they in turn would reach. By the terms of his teaching, his followers were not to behave as tyrants, "lording it over" other people, but were to be the humble servants of humanity.[14] They were to be the "salt of the earth" and the "light of the world," imparting flavor and wisdom and lasting value to all of life.[15] They were to be branches of the Vine, each an integral part of the whole, bringing forth fruit that would benefit the race, capturing souls for the Kingdom of God.[16] They were to have no part in oppression; they were to love their enemies and bless their persecutors.[17] Most particularly they were to avoid becoming involved in the kind of preoccupied religion that is unconcerned with men and society—that lays heavy burdens on men but will not lift a finger to remove those burdens.[18]

There is an often-overlooked passage in Mark's Gospel that helps to sharpen our vision of Jesus as he relates himself and his message to the social order. He is answering a complaint from the contemporary religious leaders of Galilee. It seems that his disciples were breaking the sabbath by easing their pangs of hunger with a few grains of wheat plucked from the fields as they walked through them. Jesus answered the charge by saying, "The sabbath was made on account of man, not man on account of the sabbath; so then the Son of man is Lord also of the sabbath."[19] This statement is sometimes quoted simply to show Jesus' "nonconformity to the establishment." But there is more at issue here than social nonconformism. Jesus was deliberately placing humanity, the life of man, above all social and religious considerations. He was esteeming man as the purpose for which the state and its social institutions existed. The sabbath was only the means; man was the end. The whole point of the sabbath was that it was established by God to help man by giving him one day in seven for worship and rest.

In the life of ancient Israel, of course, the ecclesiastical order and the social order were the same. When Jesus upbraided the Pharisees he was really attacking those who were exploiting society to serve their own ends. Karl Barth, the distinguished Swiss theologian, claimed in his *Epistle to the Romans* that the weaknesses of the Jewish religious establishment were the weaknesses of organized religion everywhere.[20] Instead of religion serving the people, it so often turns out that the people are serving religion. To the ancient Hebrew prophets a great deal of the religion of their day was not only oppressive to man, it was obnoxious to God. Jesus Christ stands squarely in that tradition. He would have agreed with Karl Marx that "the beginning of all criticism is the criticism of religion."[21] It was simply another way of saying, "The sabbath was made for man, and not man for the sabbath."

Jesus did not leave the matter there, for he added that he, the Son of man, was also Lord of the sabbath. Here he and Marx part company. The syllogism runs: The sabbath was devised for man's good; Jesus Christ is the Son of man; therefore Jesus Christ, who is Lord over every other aspect of man's life, is also Lord of the sabbath. Because he is Lord, he, Christ, can establish the sabbath or remove it, for the prime object of his concern is not a sacred schedule or divine institution in any case, but rather the salvation and well-being of a man's soul.

Such a blow at the complicated traditionalism of the scribes created mortal enmity in Jesus' public career. Sabbath-keeping was the heart of first-century Jewish religious life. It was regulated by detailed laws and backed by enormous prestige. Yet Jesus defended the actions of his grain-eating disciples by citing the example of the warrior David, who fed his troops at Nob with the "showbread" reserved by the priest for sacred purposes.[22] In each case human values were placed higher than ritual values—in the name of God! On the basis of a quick survey of Scripture, it can be said that the case for a Christian social conscience built around a concern for the welfare of all men has an excellent base of support.

Chapter 4

Voices out of the Long Night

The church, like the Ark of Noah, is worth saving, not for the sake of the unclean beasts and vermin that almost filled it, and probably made most noise and clamour in it, but for the little corner of rationality that was as much distressed by the stink within as by the tempest without.

—William Warburton, Bishop of Gloucester,
in a letter to a friend, June 13, 1751

Certain pages of church history thrill the socially sensitive evangelical. As he comes upon John Hus standing before the Council of Constance, or Martin Luther flinging down the gauntlet at the Diet of Worms, his spirit soars. Here, it seems to him, were the choicest grapes in the Lord's vineyard. Here were men of principle and integrity who laid their lives on the line for God and man. In the uncut pages of history, he is convinced, are the names of thousands of other heroes of truth, some of them known only to God, who kept alight the torch of true faith during the ecclesiastical blackout that fell over much of Europe.

Such a view helps to unearth the truth that in the midst of the blackout, the church itself was also a source of light. In the gentleness and compassion it spread abroad, in the restraint exercised upon human passions, in the purity of its worship, in its capacity for self-correction by the Gospel, in its cultivation of the arts and graces of life, in the outreach for lost souls, the church in its total ministry made a tremendous contribution to Western society. In fact, when the evangelical of the late twentieth century reflects on the benefit that the church of Christ through the ages has released to all mankind through its quiet, day-to-day ministries, his heart is enlarged in affection and gratitude. He holds that to belong to the true church, to acknowledge it as coming from the Spirit of God and founded by the Savior himself, to worship within its walls, is the greatest honor that life holds. Daily the believer kneels to thank his Lord from the depths of his being for his heritage of faith.

Then he looks at the record of cruelty, subterfuge, hypocrisy, and lust for power left by unworthy representatives of the visible church, and he recoils in horror. He sees some of the very ones who mounted to the top of the church's ladder stooping in the name of Christ to countenance behavior worse than that of an unbeliever or even a savage. He discovers that the pages of church history are smeared with every sin known to man. From being persecuted, the church turned persecutor; from being a vehicle of truth, it transformed itself into a vehicle of lies; from being a refuge for the poor and the outcast, it became the fortress of the established and rich. "The Church committed herself, on the highest possible principles, to a breach of the highest possible principles."[1] Too often the efforts of sincere and earnest reformers were dissolved by succeeding generations until only the external forms remained.

As the contemporary evangelical looks at it, probably the best that can be said for the two-thousand-year record of the church of Jesus Christ is that it never quite forgot him. The worst, that it frequently ignored what he said and did.

Since this study is dedicated neither to justifying the past nor to condemning it, but rather to finding resources for activating the present-day evangelical social outlook, its attitude toward history will be eclectic. Precedents will be sought to interpret a Christian role that is both germane to the present culture crisis and scripturally authentic. As early as 125 A.D. the Athenian philosopher Aristides delivered to Emperor Hadrian a defense of the faith in which he said of his fellow Christians,

They do not commit adultery or immorality; they do not bear false witness, or embezzle, nor do they covet what is not theirs. They honor father and mother, and do good to those who are their neighbors. Whenever they are judges, they judge uprightly. They do not worship idols made in the image of man. Whatever they do not wish that others should do to them, they in turn do not do; and they do not eat the food sacrificed to idols.

Those who oppress them they exhort [with the Word] and make them their friends. They do good to their enemies. Their wives, O King, are pure as virgins, and their daughters are modest. Their men abstain from all unlawful sexual contact and from impurity, in the hope of recompense that is to come in another world.

As for their bondmen and bondwomen, and their children, if there are any, they persuade them to become Christians; and when they have done so, they call them brethren without distinction.

They refuse to worship strange gods; and they go their way in all humility and cheerfulness. Falsehood is not found among them. They love one another; the widow's needs are not ignored, and they rescue the orphan from the person who does him violence. He who has gives to him who has not, ungrudgingly and without boasting. When the Christians find a stranger, they bring him to their homes and rejoice over him as a true brother. They do not call brothers those who are bound by blood ties alone, but those who are brethren after the Spirit and in God.

When one of their poor passes away from the world, each provides for his burial according to his ability. If they hear of any of their number who are imprisoned or oppressed for the name of the Messiah, they all provide for his needs, and if it is possible to redeem him, they set him free.

If they find poverty in their midst, and they do not have spare food, they fast two or three days in order that the needy might be supplied with the necessities. They observe scrupulously the commandments of their Messiah, living honestly and soberly as the Lord their God ordered them. Every morning and every hour they praise and thank God for his goodness to them; and for their food and drink they offer thanksgiving.[2]

A few years later the anonymous "Letter to Diognetus" added, "[To the Christians] every foreign land is . . . as their native country. . . . They marry . . . they beget children; but they do not destroy their offspring. They have a common table, but not a common bed."[3]

The sentiments of the second-century Christians have a universal application that would be recognized in any culture and almost any religion. Trapped in the moral upheaval now taking place, the modern evangelical would have no trouble identifying the apologists' standard as his own goal. The scriptural base is common to both. In the early centuries of church history such maxims were copied, expanded, preached, and taught wherever the church was established, although the effect of such teaching was not always evident. Too often the precept of the Nazarene was ignored: "The sabbath was made for man, not man for the sabbath."[4] Statesmen and churchmen together faced a gigantic task as they sought to build health into the socially sick residue of the Roman Empire. What they did create was a crude and complicated structure that tended toward being served rather than serving, with the result that the progress of human welfare often seemed to go into reverse. The use of torture in judicial proceedings, for example, according to the records decreased steadily in the early stages of the Christian era—only to be revived by the Inquisition. Slavery fell into gradual public disfavor—only to be replaced by serfdom. The feudal system proved as difficult a soil in which to grow the Christian social conscience as the Pax Romana had been. "In the year 1200 more than half the population of Europe was unfree, and of these unhappy serfs an enormous number belonged to the church."[5]

Nevertheless many permanent legal reforms were set in motion by Emperors Constantine (280?-337) and Justinian (483-565) that can be laid to the influence of Christianity. Licentious and cruel sports were checked; new legislation was ordered to protect the slave, the prisoner, the mutilated man, the outcast woman. Children were granted important legal rights. Infant exposure was abolished. Women were raised from a status of degradation to that of legal protection. Hospitals and orphanages were created to take care of foundlings. Personal feuds and private wars were put under restraint. In cities here and there freedom of conscience was established by law. Branding of slaves was halted. Property reforms were instituted.[6] The spirit of these changes is reflected in the growing corpus of writings of Fathers of the church, which continued to emphasize the Christian duties of almsgiving, charity, kindness to the victims of society, and good works.

Meanwhile on the edge of the church emerged certain reforming figures, such as Donatus the Great, Ratramnus of Corbie, Bérenger of Tours, Arnold of Brescia, Theresa of Avila, John Ruysbroeck, the Lollards, and their like. All were supremely Christians with consciences; all suffered for their convictions. Of equal social importance were the Brethren of the Common Life, the Friends of God, and the medieval mystics. Johannes Tauler, a Dominican mystic, could declare that a farmer spreading dung was doing work as acceptable to God as a monk at his prayers.[7] Meister Eckhart, one of the most radical of the mystics, went as far as to say, "If one were in a rapture like St. Paul, and there was a sick man needing help, I think it would be best to throw off the rapture and show love by service to the needy."[8]

Despite the valiant efforts of Christlike men in and out of the church, the great mass of Western humanity continued to grovel in poverty and wretchedness of spirit. When the Reformation came to Europe, it put magnificent emphasis on spiritual liberation, but not on social relief. Sporadic social developments did take place here and there in an effort to relieve the plight of the unfortunate. One of the more effective of these developments was the reform instituted in the canton of Zürich, Switzerland, under the leadership of the cathedral preacher, Ulrich Zwingli (1484-1531). After his ecclesiastical changes had precipitated a break with Rome, Zwingli was able, through his influence on the "Great Council" of Zürich, to effect a drastic reform in the civic attitude toward the canton's poor. Street begging was abolished in 1524, and the preacher's monastery was transformed into a "poorhouse" where each morning soup and bread were served to all who wanted it. The other monasteries and convents of Zürich were turned into schools, hospitals, and orphanages. A charity bureau was established from which various remedies, wood, wine, and food were dispensed to sick and pregnant women. Poor children were clothed and apprentices were subsidized. The register is still displayed which set forth the rules for dealing with mendicants, and the inscription at the top of the page still reads, "Be merciful, says the Lord, as your Father in heaven is merciful."[9]

Such advances were not characteristic of the sixteenth or seventeenth centuries. Radical voices were beginning to be heard in England and France, calling for sweeping revisions of the social system; but the Christian social conscience found its most creative expression not in Europe at all, but in the missionary movement that carried the Gospel around the world. The missionaries have not had a good press in the twentieth century, but with all their well-documented frailties and their unorganized zeal, they brought off an achievement whose influence and scope have never been fully assessed. These young men and women went out a hundred years or more ahead of science and technology; and if they did nothing else, they helped counteract the white man's ugly reputation for exploitation by showing another side of his nature. It can probably be said that of all those who traveled abroad during the age of imperialism, only the missionaries acted in ways that would be recognized as useful according to the exacting standards of modern social science.

All the pioneers of the modern evangelical missionary movement—Morrison of China; Schwartz, Carey, and Duff of India; Williams of the South Seas; Chalmers and Paton of New Guinea; Judson of Burma; Moffat, Livingstone, Coillard, and Mary Slessor of Africa; Veniaminov of Alaska; Gairdner of Egypt; Martyn of Persia and India; Gilmour of Mongolia and Nommensen of Sumatra—all possessed two things in common: evangelistic fervor and an active social conscience. It was inevitably so. Everywhere the far-ranging missionaries went they found themselves involved in programs of social improvement. There was black magic to be combated in Haiti, child-stealing in the Punjab, polygamy in Arabia, opium in Shantung, slavery in Madagascar, disease in Mexico, cannibalism in Micronesia, head-hunting in Borneo. Many of the missionaries failed; many stooped to immorality, "sheep-stealing," politicking, and other matters; many lost their health; but there were others who pressed on to establish God's church in a saga of amazing courage. On the west coast of Africa in the nineteenth century the average life expectancy of a newly arrived missionary was four months.

Still they came! Today the leaders of nearly every African independent nation acknowledges receiving their training skills and their motivation in Christian schools.

Over a century had elapsed after Martin Luther's death when Baron Justinian von Weltz, in the year 1664, first summoned the people of the Reformation on the continent of Europe to their missionary responsibility to non-Christian lands. Meanwhile a work began in the same century among the Indians of Massachusetts that drew the Christian world's attention to the social implications of missionary evangelism. John Eliot (1604-1690), an English schoolteacher and pastor, in a sense apotheosized the New England Christian social concern by building a model Indian community on the outskirts of the Massachusetts Bay Colony. The principles upon which Eliot functioned were sociologically sound. He learned the Algonkian language before he started; he adopted the native dress; he did not insist unduly upon cleanliness, but strove for self-respect. He answered the Indians' questions gravely and intelligently. After a three-hour teaching session there would be a distribution of apples and biscuits to the children and tobacco to the men. Eliot taught the squaws to spin and weave and garden; he established schools to instruct the young; he obtained trees for planting, taught the Indians to fence and ditch a field, and took young men into his home to instruct them in the use of carpenter's tools. Under his encouragement the Indians gave up scalping and head-tattooing, and moved into one-family wigwams. Each family received a share in the common cornfield and meadows. After ten years he established a church. It was not surprising that the Indians loved and venerated him as a father.[10]

Fifty years after Eliot's death Jean Frédéric Oberlin was born in Strasbourg, France, of Lutheran parents. He followed his family's educational pattern, receiving the doctor of philosophy degree from Strasbourg University, and found his interests leading him into the ministry. A pastor from the Vosges Mountains challenged him to serve God in the mountain villages, and he became pastor of a tiny backward, poverty-stricken parish. During the fifty years he worked in the area, he led the way in building roads, pioneered in the application of scientific agriculture, scoured Europe for seeds for his people's orchards. He founded the first kindergarten and introduced student government into the higher grades of the schools, along with botany, physics, astronomy, art, and hygiene. He published textbooks for his village students, established a circulating library, organized an auxiliary of the British and Foreign Bible Society, and promoted the circulation of the Scriptures among his people. He shielded Jews from persecution and so won the friendship of Roman Catholics that in his later years they worshiped in his church. It was fitting that after his death a town in Ohio, named for him, would become a main connection in the underground railway for slaves escaping north to Canada.[11]

By the end of the eighteenth century the Christian social conscience in England was being pricked by the worsening condition of the laboring classes in the industrial cities, and by the tragic victims of the slave traffic. About this time a young member of Parliament named William Wilberforce, converted in 1787 while on a trip to France, returned to London hoping to take holy orders. He was dissuaded from doing so by the evangelical hymn writer and former slave captain, John Newton, who urged him to serve his Lord in the House of Commons. Wilberforce thereupon determined to champion the cause of ridding his country of the slave traffic and slavery itself. He was encouraged to do so by John Wesley in a letter written three days before the latter's death.[12] Wilberforce led the fight for the rest of his own life. It took twenty years of struggle, but when the younger members of Parliament finally caught his vision, the bill to abolish slave trading swept through in the year 1807 by a vote of 283 to 16. Twenty-six years later (a month after Wilberforce died), 700,000 slaves were permanently freed throughout the British Empire, and Parliament authorized an indemnity of twenty million pounds to be paid to their former owners.[13]

What Wilberforce did for the people of Africa the seventh Lord Shaftesbury, Anthony Ashley Cooper (1801-1885), did for the people of Great Britain. Like Wilberforce, Lord Shaftesbury was a member of the Clapham Sect, a group of evangelical laymen in the London area dedicated to applying Christian principles in public life. The zeal and determination with which Shaftesbury went after the open sores of British industrial life—the chimney-sweep scandal, child labor in factories, female labor in mines and collieries, the overlong hours, the lack of safeguards and medical protection, the unhealthy working conditions—all this was matched only by the fury of his opposition, which included a good many bishops and religious types. "Many of the things which the twentieth century now prizes so much may have been born of Christian charity in the last resort, but they often had to fight the dominant voice in the church."[14] Victory eventually came; and when it did, the passage of the Ten Hours' bill in 1847 and the Factory Act in 1874 resulted largely from the effort of one man to ameliorate the condition of the working classes.[15]

Such were some of the voices out of the long night. The esteem in which their names are still held in our iconoclastic century is sufficient proof of the validity of their social conscience. They were all too few, but the torch they lighted is still blazing.

Chapter 5

The Human Factor

I knew that Christ had given me birth
To brother all the souls on earth,
And every bird and every beast
Should share the crumbs broke at the feast.

—John Masefield,
"The Everlasting Mercy"

No man is truly man until he is God's man.

—John A. Mackay

Le Play, the French engineer who discerned a century ago many of today's acute industrial problems, once asked a class what was the most important thing to come out of the mine. Various minerals were named by students; then he answered, No, the most important thing to come out of the mine was the miner.[1] The engineer identified with the words of Jesus: "The sabbath was made for man, and not man for the sabbath."[2] Recognition of the human factor has since become one of the significant and promising developments of civilization. It has most certainly wrought a revolution in modern industry.

"Human efficiency at work can only exist," a modern industrial psychologist declares, "in terms of optimal production and maximum satisfaction when the total personality is given due consideration in arranging the task and the

37

conditions of work. The disregard of a worker's capacity to feel, think, and grow is a subtle but menacing danger in breaking down his social and spiritual morale."[3]

The German studies of Henri De Man in the 1920's, and the concurrent Hawthorne experiments conducted at the Chicago plant of the Western Electric Company, revealed for the first time in a scientific way the enormous importance of interrelationships between employees in the development of work satisfactions and incentives. The Hawthorne studies showed that workers would increase their output even when the lights were dimmed to the strength of moonlight, if they thought that their labors were considered by other people to be important and significant. It was proved beyond doubt that the size of the pay envelope is not the greatest incentive to doing good work, or the chief source of work satisfaction. De Man maintained that the "acquisitive instinct may drive a man to his work, but it is hardly a constituent of joy in work. On the contrary, thought about daily bread, thought about earning, kills joy in work."[4]

The development of these pioneer studies into modern personnel methods is the result of a long, uphill battle of the human race against entrenched economic forces that refused to yield power or to acknowledge the right of a man to be himself. Even at the time Le Play was teaching, millions of people in the Western world were being trapped in the poisonous discharge of the industrial revolution. Long hours, low wage scales, unhealthy working conditions, overcrowded squalid housing, racial bigotry, managerial exploitation, and corrupt municipal politics all contributed to the social sickness. The indigent farmer's boy drifted to the big city and was trapped in the tentacles of giant production. The immigrant father arrived in America from Europe under a work contract that virtually indentured him for years to a low-paying corporation. The Negro plantation worker obtained his political freedom at the price of a bloody civil war, but his economic problems remained insoluble.

It has been noted that certain Christians have been sufficiently sensitive to the mass misery to attempt to alleviate it.[5] Their expressions of interest and concern came to be known in America in the nineteenth century as the "social gospel."[6] Dr. Timothy Smith of the University of Minnesota has rendered a service to the church by unearthing a little-known fact about the social gospel: it took its roots not in religious "liberalism" or skepticism, but in the evangelical revival.[7] The social gospel has been under theological attack for so long by orthodoxy that most people are stunned by Dr. Smith's claims. His documentation, however, is irrefutable. When the social gospel first appeared it was a serious evangelical effort to apply the compassion of Christ to the lives of men.

The evangelical preacher, the revivalist, the mass evangelist, carried the doctrines of holiness and Christian perfection into the seamy aspects of the day. They revealed a boundless passion for the welfare of humanity. Anything that stood in the way of making America great—and Christian—they opposed.[8] Thus they spoke frequently for the friendless, the jobless, the drunkard, the illiterate, the Indian and the Negro, the widow and the orphan. In eastern and midwestern United States the evangelicals were often drawn into the struggle against slavery. Calvinist and Methodist alike were giving spiritual support to the abolition movement in the 1840's and 1850's.

The town of Oberlin, Ohio, founded by Charles G. Finney as a college for the training of evangelists, became (as was mentioned earlier) a main connecting point on the "underground railroad."[9] President Finney himself was not above hiding fugitive slaves in his attic. The famed lawyer-evangelist stumped the state addressing antislavery societies, and provided as many supporters of the Negro's cause as did William Lloyd Garrison, the abolitionist.[10] Finney proclaimed a sanctifying Gospel that would, he prayed, save souls, revive the church, reconstruct society, and put an end to slavery and poverty. With him in the work were many evangelists, such as Joshua Leavitt, Samuel Schmucker, Jacob Knapp, Theodore Dwight Weld, the Grimké sisters, and others.

After the Civil War and the Reconstruction period the character of the social gospel changed. New leaders appeared and joined their sympathies to the growing working-class movement. Such actions aroused the ire of well-to-do conservative elements in the established churches. These elements suspected "deviations" not only in the preachers' sociology but in their theology, and the suspicions proved to be correct.

It is not the purpose of this volume to make a historical appraisal of the popular leaders of America's social gospel movement, or to weigh their theological errors against their positive accomplishments in awakening the social conscience of the churches. Scripture warns us that God alone is judge. These men did what more orthodox men should have done, but were too blind or too timid to do.[11] They challenged the economic royalism of the time; they struggled against poverty and misery; they defended the right of workers to organize and to strive for a better standard of living; they insisted that Christianity had more to offer a laboring man than an exhortation "not to be drunk and disorderly in his leisure hours, and to come to church on Sundays."[12]

Just how the church often practiced its quietism is illustrated by Walter Rauschenbusch in a story he says was told him by a Toronto health officer. When the Ontario health officials found dirt in the milk coming in from the farms, according to the officer, they emptied the cans and marked

them with large red labels. This proved a moral irritant to
the farmer, who did not care to drive his team to the railroad station and find his friends chuckling over the red
labels on his cans. One day a member of a devout Christian
sect discovered his cans so labeled, and swore a worldly
oath. His church was one that did not believe in swearing,
even in law courts. The farmer was brought before his
church and excluded—"not," as Rauschenbusch points out,
"for introducing cow dung into the intestines of babies, but
for expressing his beliefs in the damnation of the wicked
in a non-theological way."[13]

Such a story has an almost New Testament ring to it.
One can fairly hear Jesus of Nazareth saying to the careless
farmer, "You should not have neglected this (keeping the
name of the Lord out of your list of expletives) but should
also have done the other (delivered pure milk)." The evangelical Christian hears a story of this nature and breathes
a heartfelt "amen." His instinctive concern for human values
and his knowledge of the mind of Christ lend support to
such an emphasis. Then he discovers to his dismay that the
same people who are so concerned to affirm social change
are also inexplicably denying the reality of spiritual change
in persons.

A heart-cry of the evangelical as he faces the crisis of our
own day continues to be: Why does the move toward social
involvement seem to require a rejection of Biblical Christianity? Why must the one accompany the other? The Gospel
of Jesus Christ was in the first century a revolutionary message, miracles and all. It still is! What is there in the present
age that seems to make it mandatory for a man to move
from orthodoxy to atheism before he can be taken seriously
in his quest for the good of humanity? In 1908 the following
statement of social principles was adopted by the Federal
Council of Churches of Christ in America:

The Federal Council . . . stands:

For equal rights and complete justice for all men in all stations of life.

For the abolition of child-labor.

For such regulation of the conditions of toil for women as shall safeguard the physical and moral health of the community.

For the suppression of the "Sweating System."

For the gradual and reasonable reduction of the hours of labor to the lowest practicable point, and for that degree of leisure for all which is the condition of the highest human life.

For a release from employment one day in seven.

For the right of all men to the opportunity for self-maintenance, a right ever to be wisely and strongly safeguarded against encroachments of every kind.

For the right of workers to some protection against the hardships often resulting from the swift crises of industrial change.

For a living wage as a minimum in every industry, and for the highest wage that each industry can afford.

For the protection of the worker from dangerous machinery, occupational disease, injuries and mortality.

For suitable provision for the old age of the workers and for those incapacitated by injury.

For the principle of conciliation and arbitration in industrial dissensions.

For the abatement of poverty.

For the most equitable division of the products of industry that can ultimately be devised.[14]

The place of church pronouncements on social issues will be considered in a later chapter.[15] Most, if not all, of the principles set forth in the 1908 statement are now part of the accepted way of life in Western countries. They can hardly be called "radical" any longer. Many evangelicals who are sharply critical of recent trends in the social theory of the National Council of Churches would agree that the 1908 statement is a good expression of Christian social concern. Does it, then, require a disbelief in the virgin birth of Jesus Christ? No. Does it imply that salvation lies elsewhere than through the vicarious sacrifice of the Son of God on the cross? No. Does it deny the blood atonement, the Resurrection or the Second Advent? No. Whether the men who wrote the statement believed in these cardinal tenets of faith is not the question at the moment. It is, rather: Does there need to be a denial of evangelical truth before such a social position can be adopted?

Were it a matter of Communist influence, an entirely different construction would be put on the whole issue. A chief ideological tenet of the Marxists is the boast that they will, through sheer determined effort and single-minded purpose, achieve their own salvation in this life. They ridicule "bourgeois morality," and consider the social conscience only a tool for gaining and keeping power. But are any such ideas planted in the 1908 statement? No. Did any evangelical Christians sign it? Undoubtedly. Yet the later developments of social theory in the Federal Council ran concurrent with a decreasing interest in Biblical Christianity on the part of its leaders and a decreasing inclination to ascribe final authority to the Scriptures.

Partly as a result of this defection, there came about a strange joining of interests: a rapprochement between evangelical Christianity and economic reaction; between those who sought to turn the world upside down with the Gospel and those who were determined to preserve the world as it was, warts and all. Social conservatism has tried many times over the centuries to neutralize evangelical theology. Amos fought it at Bethel, and others have struggled against it since. The most innocent alliances have been used to perpetuate the status quo. Mr. Wanamaker was a supporter of

Mr. Moody; Mr. Rockefeller was interested in Billy Sunday. There is no implication that the evangelists adopted the politics of their wealthy friends, or that the latter in turn interfered in any way with the clear presentation of the Gospel. The evangelists continued to serve God and man with tremendous effectiveness. Thousands of converts were reclaimed for society. New channels of social welfare were opened up under the impetus of Christian conviction.

And yet—there was a subtle difference. From the vantage point of our own day it looks as if something happened to render opaque the social vision of many an evangelist. The desperate, wasting plight of the poor slid out of his purview. He saw the good that God was doing, the souls saved for eternity; what he did not realize was that the God of Amos and Isaiah and James was calling him, as a Christian and a responsible person, to say and do something about the social blight around him. As a result, the Christian zeal created by the revival failed to make a successful frontal attack on the acute problems of the day. Evangelist Sam Jones closed down 27 bars by actual count in Knoxville, Tennessee, but left untouched the gigantic questions of segregation and poverty.[16] Yet the Bible deals with all three issues.

A serious contributing factor to the paralyzing of the evangelical's social conscience in the past hundred years has been the uproar over the Bible. Many people of our time are unaware of the battle that the evangelicals of America and Britain were thrust into following the publication of Darwin's *Origin of Species* in 1859. Much of the controversy carried on by the believers was needless and foredoomed to failure; it consisted of efforts to defend lost causes which the Bible never set forth, and which Christ himself never championed. But there was one cause that was and still is dear to the heart of every evangelical Christian, and that is the integrity of Holy Scripture.

The attack on the text of the Bible was mounted on several fronts. Darwin, Huxley, Spencer, and others based their historical conclusions on their investigations of the natural sciences. Strauss, Ewald, Graf, Wellhausen, and other German scholars developed a system of radical internal criticism of the Old Testament. Marx, Haeckel, Durkheim, and others chose the sociological approach to religion. The Freudian school applied the insights of psychology to the study of the behavior of religiously inclined patients. All managed to agree at one point: the Biblical documents were scientifically unreliable and filled with erroneous material.

Those Christian apologists who continued to maintain in the face of the assault that the Old and New Testaments were the authentic revelation of God himself found that they were backed to the wall. The forces ranged against them were unbelievably powerful. They themselves had few human resources with which to fight back and expose peremptory scientific conclusions (such as the Hittite error) or frauds (such as the Piltdown hoax). They were not, as a rule, at home in the cognate languages of the Middle East. They had little scientific, scholastic, or philosophical training. As a result they spent a great deal of time floundering in water over their heads and appearing as a laughingstock in the eyes of the intellectual world.

In Darwin the evangelicals found a more formidable opponent than all of his contemporaries together, because he went straight to the matter of origins. What the English botanist seemed to be saying, in his mild-mannered way, was that man was not a spiritual being at all; rather he was a complex organism, atavistic in nature, with certain refinements derived by natural selection from the lower forms of life from which he was descended. Today there are outstanding scientists who are challenging Darwin's whole fabric of interpretation, and some of them are evangelical Christians.[17]

Other experts are giving Wellhausen, Haeckel, Spencer, and others a reexamination that has canceled out some of their basic conclusions that seemed so assured in the nineteenth century. Freud's attacks on religion are being dismissed even by Freudians as the least useful of his writings.

Fifty years ago no such expert criticism was forthcoming. The battle was left—or so it seemed—to the orthodox preachers and writers who just "believed in the Bible." At the very time when they should have been actively and helpfully involved in working out the huge problems of a society in transition, and speaking up for the rights of man as Jesus did, the evangelical Christians were being driven by the heavy artillery of the critics to consolidate their defenses around the Bible. Valuable spiritual ammunition which could have been put to constructive use was being used up in denunciation and rhetoric. Energy and vitality were drained by argument.

Today's evangelicals look back with affection upon the stouthearted zealots who took up cudgels for the purity of the faith. The chinks in their armor are showing today; their lack of graduate study is all too obvious. Yet they stood up under fire to witness to the cause of Biblical truth, and that cause today is on more solid ground than ever. Seen in evangelical perspective, the weakness of the Bible defender of the recent past was not so much his premises or his logic as his failure to look out for the needs of his neighbor. He was too often blinded by all the smoke from the theological brush fires and unable to see what was happening to his world. The social conscience of the evangelical went into rigor mortis.

Chapter 6

Plumb Bob on the Saints

It is not the unfrocking of a priest, the unmitering of a bishop . . . that will make us a happy nation; no, if other things as great in the church and in the rule of life both economical and political be not looked into and reformed, then we have looked so long upon the blaze that Zwingli and Calvin hath beaconed up to us that we are stark blind.

—John Milton, *Areopagitica*

In early 1947 a converted young newspaperman-turned-professor, armed with a doctorate from Northern Baptist Theological Seminary, wrote a series of articles for a now defunct Michigan organ known as the *Religious Digest*. The series was considered too provocative for the magazine, so it was issued instead by the publishing house of Eerdmans as a thin volume of essays. The book dropped like a bomb into the peaceful summer Bible conference atmosphere of the postwar evangelical community. It was entitled *The Uneasy Conscience of Modern Fundamentalism,* and its author was Carl Ferdinand Howard Henry, who nine years later was to become the founding editor of *Christianity Today.*

The positive effect of Dr. Henry's book was to awaken a few evangelical leaders to the fact that their movement, beloved of God, had lost some of the social passion of the Bible and the sensitivity of Jesus Christ to human need. "There is a growing awareness in Fundamentalist circles," wrote Henry, "that, despite the orthodox insistence upon revelation and redemption, evangelical Christianity has become increasingly inarticulate about the social reference of the Gospel. . . . Fundamentalism is wondering just how it is that a world-changing message narrowed its scope to the changing of isolated individuals. . . . The failure of the evangelical movement to react favorably on any widespread front to campaigns against social evils has led, finally, to a suspicion on the part of non-evangelicals that there is something in the very nature of Fundamentalism which makes a world ethical view impossible."[1]

The young prophet's proposals toward remedying the failure were just as outspoken: "Though the modern crisis is not basically political, economic or social—fundamentally it is religious—yet evangelicalism must be armed to declare the implications of its proposed religious solution for the politico-economic and sociological context of modern life."[2]

That the social evils of the modern era have by no means been utterly neglected by the evangelicals is a point that cannot be stated too often. Social historians are well aware that for over two hundred years, under the impetus of John Wesley and the evangelical revival, Christian eleemosynary institutions and "works of mercy" have been proliferating in Europe and America. City rescue missions, societies for the blind; hospitals, sanitaria, orphanages, homes for the aged, ragged schools, and centers of healing; YMCA's, institutions for the mentally retarded, for the blind, for fallen girls, for widows, for prisoner rehabilitation; for the protection of animals; and a host of similar operations came into being to meet the growing needs. The Roman Catholic Church, of course, developed its own charity outlets. Societies and movements such as the Salvation Army, the Church Army, the Volunteers of America, and the St. Vincent de Paul Society leaped into the breach and still bear testimony to the warm and compassionate hearts of Christian people.[3]

For over two hundred years Christian laymen have toiled in the chambers of government to push through reforms that would lift the status of the downtrodden, the underprivileged, the overworked, the underpaid, and the racially rejected. American clergymen were among the original group that formed the Knights of Labor. English clergymen joined in the Chartist movement, seeking to improve the lot of the working class. James Keir Hardie, a Scottish miner who as a young man preached Christ in the churches of the Evangelical Union, became the founder of the British Labour Party. Christoph Blumhardt, an ordained minister of the Lutheran Church of Württemburg, Germany, served two terms in the legislature on a working-class platform and was voted out of the church as a result.

Yet historical judgments are based upon total effect, and in the midst of the appalling destitution created by the industrial revolution, the combined efforts of all Christian agencies were fragmentary. It is one thing to attack the general problem of industrial poverty through a national policy; it is another to engage in small-scale religious philanthropy. Big city prostitution, narcotics, gambling, crime, unemployment, alcoholism, and disease were matters simply too great for the resources of a storefront rescue mission. So the church as a whole drew its skirts aside; the faithful members shook their heads and said there was little they could do about the wretched social conditions except pray. They forgot the strong words that God spoke to the people of Israel on a day of solemn fasting:

> Is not this the fast that I choose:
>   to loose the bonds of wickedness,
>   to undo the thongs of the yoke,
> to let the oppressed go free,

and to break every yoke?
Is it not to share your bread with the hungry,
    and bring the homeless poor into your house;
when you see the naked, to cover him,
    and not to hide yourself . . . ?[4]

On such a counterreading, the social impress of evangelical Christianity between 1860 and 1960, apart from its missionary outreach, must be judged a failure. Tested by the words of Jesus Christ himself, it was a failure of love. There was too much wrong with the world, and too little was being said and done about it. "Behold, I am setting a plumb line in the midst of my people Israel. . . . I know how many are your transgressions, and how great are your sins."[5]

And yet the churches were not idle; the Spirit of God was at work in individuals, and wave after wave of revival was experienced. Many congregations on both sides of the Atlantic came to know genuine spiritual awakening. Concern for probity and conduct was renewed; a vigorous infusion of Biblical morality became the misnamed "Puritan conscience" that held the English-speaking civilization together down to our own time. But the issue under discussion is not evangelism or revival or morality in the narrow sense, vital as these matters are to every evangelical Christian. Jesus did not command his followers only to evangelize their neighbors and to set an example of good behavior. He told them to *love* their neighbors. When the witnessing Christian fails to love, and to express that love in existential situations, he throws away much of his testimony. Zeal for the house of the Lord, warned the Apostle James, is no excuse for ignoring the condition of the people.

There is no use trying to fight back with countercharges of heresy. Beating a theological horse, however justified, will not get the evangelicals out of their predicament. God can deal with heresy; but what can he do with men who profess

the faith and ignore the ghettoes of life? "If . . . ye have
respect to him that weareth the gay clothing, and say unto
him, Sit thou here in a good place; and say to the poor, Stand
thou there, or sit here under my footstool: Are ye not then
partial in yourselves, and are become judges of evil
thoughts?"[6] What the evangelical of the sixties wants to do
is to return the church to its historic Biblical position of
concern for society. The thousand missionary and church
leaders who signed the "Wheaton Declaration of 1966" con-
fessed, "We have sinned grievously. We are guilty of an unscriptural isolation from the world that too often keeps us
from honestly facing and coping with its concerns. We have
failed to apply scriptural principles to such problems as
racism, war, population explosion, poverty, family disin-
tegration, social revolution and communism."[7]

When the evangelical rises from his knees with a vision of
Christ's compassion for the world, however, he faces a problem. Not only is he handicapped by inexperience and by
an unsatisfactory immediate past; he is also hobbled by the
world's suspicion, which is not entirely based on false sup-
positions. Many socially minded people with sincere desire
for the good of humanity carry a long-standing conviction
that if a "brother" has been genuinely converted to Christ,
has "got religion," then his social conscience is dead. He has
become as the priest and the Levite in the Parable of the
Good Samaritan. He may be of some use to God, they say
(although they cannot imagine what that would be) but he
is certainly of no use to man.

The evangelical also faces a practical difficulty: where does
he take hold? For he finds that in recent years the field has
been preempted by others. Do-gooders (and -not-so-gooders)
are all over the place, operating under every kind of banner
or no banner, some to plant and build up, some to break
down and pluck up that which is planted. They are zealously

dedicated to every conceivable kind of cause from Maoism to Nazism, and from LSD to cancer research. Furthermore, the social work once carried out by his forebears has drifted into other hands. Charity institutions are increasingly coming under the control of secular boards of trustees. Christmas baskets have been replaced by government unemployment checks. Church-related schools are becoming more distantly related year by year, as they reach for Federal subsidies. Overseas the social work formerly performed by missionaries has been invaded not only by expanding national governments but by the Peace Corps concept, which has sent young men and women of social vision from a dozen countries into the bush.

Further, some of the radical voices now attacking such problems as thermonuclear energy, automation, civil rights, birth control, alcoholism, homosexuality, and obscenity are shouting that there is only one possible position for a normal human being to take on each issue. If the evangelical wishes to wade into the social stream, if he wishes to become "involved," he is told that he had better make sure he chooses the right side. Any other choice is a vote against humanity! To a sincere Christian, however, the workable approach to social questions is an approach that reflects the mind of Christ. His ethical principles are drawn not from the latest consensus but from the commandments of God. As the Wheaton evangelicals expressed it, they "are increasingly convinced that they must involve themselves in the great social problems men are facing." They are "concerned for the needs of the whole man, because of their Lord's example, his constraining love, their identity with the human race, and the challenge of their evangelical heritage." Therefore they urged their brethren "to stand openly and firmly for racial equality, human freedom, and all forms of social justice. . . ."[8]

The evangelical of today thinks of himself as conservative at many points, because he believes that the values of faith and life are worth conserving. At the same time he refuses to turn into a tool in the hands of oppression and privilege. Perhaps in the immediate past some of his prototypes were unable to distinguish between conservatism and reaction. The contemporary evangelical is not about to repeat the mistake. On the other hand, he feels no requirement to draw his understanding of human need from the doctrinaire socialists of France (Proudhon, Fourier, *et al.*), or the dialecticians of modern Russia, China, or Cuba. The insights of Scripture he considers adequate for a genuine social ethic.

To sum up, the evangelical emerges from his Rip van Winkle sleep to find that the issues are already being defined for him. Even as he opens his Bible and draws on the spiritual resources that are available, he is tossed on the horns of a dilemma. For if he chooses one position, he chances being branded as a Himmler-type reactionary; but if he chooses the opposite, he risks being herded with atheistic pinks and homosexuals. If he proposes to make the Bible his touchstone and guide, he is engulfed by a torrent of literature purporting to show that the Bible's social teaching sanctions everything from state lotteries and genocide to ship-picketing, blood donations to the Viet Cong, and tossing Molotov cocktails at heads of state. If he withdraws to seek the witness of the Spirit and the whole counsel of God, he is cited as a quietist and obscurantist. Hyperactive churchmen hold him up as an example of the irrelevance of faith to works.

So the risks are great; nevertheless, they must be taken. Somehow, somewhere, the love of Christ has to shine into these cloudy and obscure matters. Evangelicals will make mistakes; they will sometimes find themselves lined up on opposite sides of the same issue for identical reasons; they will become confused by the subtlety of the issues involved and by the fine shadings of right and wrong. Who is to decide, for example, which hours are the best for the work shifts in a taconite mill? Who is to determine that job security is less important, or more important, than technological advance? Many concerned laymen—those who are really making their presence and their witness felt in the secular world—are already wrestling with these issues. The evangelicals can pass by on the other side no longer. Somewhere in between the anthills of Marxism and the iron fist of Fascism is a Christian position, reflecting the mind of our living Lord and the justice and integrity of God; and they have got to find it.

Chapter 7

The Call and the Calling

With him ther was a Plowman, was his brother,
That hadde y-lad of dong ful many a fother. . . .
God loved he best with al his holë herte
At allë tymes, thogh him gamëd or smerte,
And thanne his neighëbour right as him-selve.
He woldë thresshe, and ther-to dyke and delve,
For Christes sake, for every povrë wight
Withouten hyre, if it lay in his might.

—Chaucer,
Prologue to *The Canterbury Tales*

The primary goal of the Christian life, according to the New Testament, is to know the will of God and to do it. Invariably Scripture interprets that will in terms of human beings. When Christ sent out disciples, he sent them to people. They were to witness to people, to heal people, to offer heart and hand to people. If they were called to suffer for their faith, they were to do so on behalf of people. They were to follow the example of their Lord, who died neither for truth nor virtue nor any other cause, but for people.

The way a Christian goes about fulfilling the divine will among his fellows is known in Scripture as his vocation. The English word "calling," for which "vocation" is a synonym, came into use at the time of the Coverdale translation of the Bible in 1535. It is based on the Greek word κλῆσις. At one

55

point in the 1611 King James New Testament (Ephesians 4:1) κλῆσις is translated "vocation." The latter word has gone through many changes since the Reformation; so many, in fact, that W. G. Symons complains, "The trouble about the word vocation is to find out what it means."[1] Murray's *Oxford Dictionary* defines it as "action on the part of God of calling a person," and then distinguishes three principal types of call: (1) the call to a special mission or function; (2) the call to salvation, and (3) the divinely determined secular station or calling in which one serves. The variations on these definitions are so subtle that no dictionary can adequately represent them. In the fields of education, industry, and trade, the terms vocation and calling have developed into convenient synonyms for "occupation." In recent years they have been put to work not only in school and mart but in the technical laboratory. Education research has developed an entire science to which it has given the name of vocational guidance. Industrial research has performed a similar task with vocational selection. Meanwhile the *Catholic Encyclopedia* continues to identify a vocation as the restricted ministry of a priest, a monk, or a nun. So the idea of a sacred vocation and a secular vocation is retained, but the Biblical concept of the sacred at work in the secular has been obscured.

In the Scriptures the call of God becomes the specific means of implementing the will of God; and that call is never divorced from people. Abraham was called to found a nation; Moses was called to deliver a nation; Jonah was called—twice—to bring a nation to repentance. The Book of Jonah is really a sociological classic, for the son of Amittai held the same attitude toward the people of Nineveh that some missionaries have been criticized for holding toward the "heathen." Jonah did not care about Assyrians, but he was totally wrapped up in the problem of his conscience before God. In a similar way evangelists and missionaries have sometimes been charged with being more interested in

religious duties than in people.[2] That road is a perilous one.
The Apostle Paul realized from the moment of his conversion
that his task was to spread the Good News among Greek-
speaking people all over the known world. His letters are evidence that he did not consider it a duty to be discharged but
a love to be cultivated and intimately shared.

Today there is a need to restore the word vocation to its
Biblical significance. It is true that whoever speaks for God
is engaged in the service of God; and that every time a Christian tells someone about the purpose of God revealed on
Calvary, he is fulfilling his vocation. But the Lord does not
call half a man. He does not press a man's mouth into service
and ignore his hands and feet. Spraying the universe with
words is not the same thing as communicating with another
human being. To be called means putting the whole personality into orbit for God, in the way that is most effective for
for God among men. It means a complete utilization of one
man for another. But where, and when, and in what manner
does he go about fulfilling this vocation?

The Biblical answer to "where" is wherever people are.
The "when" is determined by the sovereignty of God and
the working of the Holy Spirit. Without spiritual preparation of the soil by the Lord himself, the best of the Christian's
efforts to sow seeds of faith are still bound to yield nothing
but wood, hay, and stubble. But there are certain guidelines
that can be established. The ordinary man moves in a fairly
circumscribed sphere that embraces his home, the homes of
relatives and friends, one or two places of leisure-time activity, occasional public gatherings—and his place of work.
In all these places the evangelical is called to live for the
Lord. Because it is so uncharted, as an area of potential witness and as a field for the evangelical's social conscience, it
would be well to pay some attention to the Christian's vocation in the place where men work.

Work today has become the most important thing in life

for millions of people. An industrial society tends to gravitate increasingly, not about the store, the church, or the inn, but about the factory. The one fixed geographical locus is the "plant," the house of the machine. It determines the locality of residence and social activity. It may even determine the shape of mountains and the course of rivers. Thus work comes to assume an overwhelming importance for men. The farmer may interrupt his spring plowing to observe the Lord's Day, but the Bessemer furnace that takes weeks and months to heat cannot be left untended for a moment. Instead of the machine serving man, it is becoming increasingly evident that man is being forced to serve the machine. Man therefore has to bring to his work the full scope of his efficient powers. Thousands of laborers in office and factory have almost no social intercourse outside of their work. Work extracts from them the best part of the energy they expend in a twenty-four-hour period.

On the job the Christian's vocation acquires special significance, if for no other reason than that he can be seen for what he is and not for what he says he is. All the impressive statements he makes in leisure hours can be validated or negated by his conduct at the desk or at the bench. His testimony takes on a new and significant aspect as his fellow workers watch him react to the conditions they face: temptation, unfairness, exploitation, corruption, danger, ennui, abuse, and all the rest. Verbalizing may or may not be a part of his witness during working hours. A steel worker on a scaffolding is hardly expected to be a professional evangelist. Verbal evangelism at the wrong moment has been known to disrupt work and even to jeopardize human life. The Marxist may feel he can propagandize on the job to the neglect of his task; the Christian who lives by the Bible cannot do so. There is "a time for silence and a time for speech."[3]

But there are many opportunities for a Christian to witness in connection with his work. An excellent illustration
—and one in which the evangelical witness has been con-
spicuously absent—is provided by the organized labor movement. To many respectable churchgoers of the past there
was something almost indecent about the lowly members of
the nation's labor force banding together in an effort to improve their lot in life and to claim a greater share of the
national product. They considered that the labor movement
smacked of ingratitude, disrespect, sedition, and worldliness.
Organized labor has had to contend in its struggle not only
against management and ownership, but against the very institution whose Founder was a carpenter. The voting record
of English bishops in the House of Lords during the past
hundred and fifty years on labor and factory reform issues
could hardly be construed, by any stretch of the imagination,
as "good news to the poor." But the Church of England was
not the sole offender. Some evangelical students of prophecy
in America have been known to contend that the "locusts"
in the Book of Revelation, with "faces like men" and "power
like the power of scorpions,"[4] were the labor unions. The
unions got the message, and workingmen began to leave the
churches in droves, creating what Pope Leo XIII called the
great scandal of the nineteenth century.

The Bible considers a man's work honorable and necessary.[5] It contains no injunction against the right to strike,
nor does it forbid the right of workers to band together for
purposes of mutual assistance.[6] To condemn the millions of
men and women in organized labor simply because they are
organized is contrary to the mind of Christ as revealed in the
New Testament. Furthermore, if one is to reproach the
unions for elevating a notorious man to leadership, one
should also reproach industry for producing price-fixing
executives, and government for producing men who take

bribes, and the church for producing Judas. *For there is no difference; for all have sinned.*[7]

What can be done in the name of Christ to help men, in or out of unions? That is the vocation to which the evangelical is summoned. He is not to get into the argument so much as to get into the act for Christ. The labor unions offer a tremendous field for sharing the good news of salvation. So do the echelons of management and commerce. But vocation also means social involvement. It means ministering to people where they are, by word and deed, in the Savior's name. "Make the application of Christianity to present-day life a reality," said Keir Hardie, the father of the British Labour Party, "and none will support it with more zeal than the workers."[8] A Christian carrying his cross must expect to make contact with social issues.

Today automation is wiping out 35,000 jobs every week in America. Dr. Kenneth Boulding of the University of Michigan predicts that the world of the future will require less than 10 per cent of the population to produce all the basic commodities. Will that result in more leisure time? More moonlighting? Or a guaranteed annual wage? Dr. Boulding's prediction must stand against the well-known fact that the world's food production must be doubled by 1980 and trebled by the year 2000 if there is to be any improvement at all in the diet of mankind. Should the evangelical be tempted to conclude that such problems are "outside the Gospel," he had better study again the accounts of Jesus' feeding of the five thousand and related texts. George Mac-Leod likes to describe the service of Holy Communion as symbolizing man's central problem of existence: the distribution of bread.[9]

Even while it has achieved its high level of efficiency, the industrial revolution has multiplied the miseries and frustrations of millions of little people. Anyone can make a list of grievances: the feelings of loneliness, of insignificance, of anonymity, monotony, triviality; of staleness, bitterness, uselessness, hopelessness. Add to them the occupational diseases and psychological damage caused by industry in the human body, and one is inclined to ask whether "progress" is worth it.

> But as for the mills of men
> Don't be harnessed to them.
> The dead give ships and engines, cinema,
>   radio and gramophone,
> And they say: Now, behold, you are living
>   the great life! . . .
> As you know, it is a complete lie.
> You are all going dead and corpse pale
> Listening in to the lie.
> Spit it out. . . .[10]

Well and good for Martin Luther to say that a milkmaid could milk cows to the glory of God. Luther helped to liberate the concept of God's call from the cloister, and he is honored for it; but can a man operate a hundred milking machines to the glory of God? If so, how? When a minor functionary in a mammoth computer operation comes to Christ, does he find his work taking on new meaning through a sense of divine vocation? Yes, but not in the way that might be expected. The answers are not to be found in fanciful idealism, but some resources are to be found in Christian realism. Perhaps a story will illustrate.

The author once related to the late Emil Brunner the tale of the three men working on a cathedral, each of whom was asked by a bystander what he was doing. The first replied, "I'm carrying these stones"; the second said, "I'm earning my wages"; and the third, "I am building a cathedral." That story, noticeably cast in a medieval framework, has been told hundreds of times in Sunday-school assemblies to illustrate the meaning of vocation. Yet it means almost nothing to a machine age, which builds not cathedrals but bigger machines. Professor Brunner's comment was, "It is a romantic fable. I would prefer the second answer. The Lord calls a man to be a provider. A Christian can always find meaning in his wages, for they provide food and shelter for human beings."[11]

There are many aspects of vocation that affect the Christian's daily stint. The quality of workmanship, the kind of service given to the public, the relationships between employees and between employer and employee, all are brought within earshot, so to speak, of the call to discipleship. The choice of a career by a young man or young woman of evangelical convictions can never be determined solely by an occupational interest inventory. A guidance counselor who seeks to determine whether a student's interests are "verbal," "manipulative," or "computational" can only be trusted so far. Vocation sometimes consists of God's laying his hands on the wrong man! It is good to know that a young person is interested in opportunity for advancement, pleasant people to work with, good hours, prestige, certainty of continuous employment, easy work, opportunity to work inside or out, and so on. None of these, however, mean much when the divine constraint puts a man to work among people in the full dimensions of the New Testament.

William Temple hinted that the concept of vocation may even solve ethical problems that cannot otherwise be unraveled.[12] It can secure the conscience in the performance of its duty. It can forge a connecting link between theology and ethics.[13] "The idea of vocation," declares N. H. G. Robinson, "is the central concept of Christian ethics. [It recognizes] both that love is the fulfilling of the law and that the practice of love is never merely the application to concrete situations of a preconceived principle, but is always potentially a fresh revelation of God's will and God's grace."[14]

To know the will of God and to do it seems a fairly simple challenge and call on Sunday morning; on Monday morning it is something else. It is to the Monday vocational arena that the disciple is being called by the Lord of the church. No Christian is expected to parade his religion, but neither is he to mask what he believes. Jesus said, "Let your light so shine before men that they may see your good works and glorify your Father which is in heaven."[15] That means in part that the Christian wins acceptance for his testimony on the job by the way he works. "The medium is the message," as Marshall McLuhan tells us. Jesus sold Peter in part at least by surpassing him in his own trade as a fisherman.[16]

The Hawthorne experiments enormously heightened the importance of the informal working group in the process of production.[17] The social atmosphere of the working group is now stressed in industry as directly related to output. Relations between such personnel today are being encouraged rather than restricted. Here is an important field of witness of which the church is only dimly aware. Similarly immense vocation values are to be found in the postwar institution known as the "coffee break." Leisure-time activities, organized around common professional interests, offer the Christian opportunities to testify to that which God has called him to do. Driving to work is as much a part of his vocation as anything the Christian does all day long. The behavior of motorists in a line of traffic can show, as quickly as any other situation, what the Grace of God really means to an evangelical.

The spirit of man, said the wise one, is the candle of the Lord.[18] As long as that candle remains unlit man toils in darkness. His soul is dead. His human equation does not work out, his melody is played in a minor key. But once the taper of the soul is lighted, all is changed. The working hours can become radiant. The work itself can acquire meaning.

And if that does not happen, then the hours away from work will still provide the time and occasion for a man to serve his Lord. Thus the Christian's sense of vocation becomes a divine summons to a strong and fruitful life. It is an event in eternity actualized in time.

Chapter 8

Interlocking Freedom

To restrict the powers of an arbitrary government; to free the individual from the authority of an arbitrary church; to reinterpret the common law to establish a society of free individuals; and to reshape society to fit the needs of free men in all the aspects of the social need: these constituted the purposes of Puritanism.

—H. G. Plum

Freedom ranks after life itself as the quintessence of the human experience. Freedom defines the man; it stamps the divine image upon him. In varying contexts and differing degrees, such a view has been traditionally held in the Western world. The evangelical Christian, claiming a distinctive heritage, insists that he will yield to no one in his devotion to freedom; yet he too has his qualifying conditions. The most important is his understanding of his status as a citizen of two worlds, this one and the next.

On the Liberty Bell in Philadelphia's Independence Hall is cast a verse from Leviticus: "Proclaim liberty throughout the land to all the inhabitants thereof."[1] The meaning is secular rather than sacred. The commandment is part of the regulations affecting the Year of Jubilees which (as was mentioned earlier[2]) was a plan to rectify chronic imbalances in the Hebrew economy. Every fifty years, according to the code, all who had lost property were to have it restored to them, and all who had fallen into slavery were to be freed and permitted to return home. The "liberty" involved was political and legal. So far as is known, the system was unique in the ancient world.

When Jesus entered the synagogue at Nazareth he read from the scroll of Isaiah the words, "The Spirit of the Lord is upon me . . . to proclaim liberty to the captives, and the opening of the prison to those who are bound."[3] Critics who assume the Scriptures to be quietistic on the issue of slavery need to reexamine those words. Who were the captives? Who were the prisoners? Authorities advise us that they were in fact slaves.[4] Captivity in the ancient world was simply another word for slavery. According to the *Iliad* the prisoners who were captured in war were retained as slaves, or sold, or held for ransom by the captor.[5] Thus Isaiah's prophecy referred to a postwar slave condition existing among the Jews in the Middle East, possibly in the sixth century before Christ.

Jesus took Isaiah's exciting words, which had such strong political significance when they were written, and imparted to them a new dimension. The interpretation of Jesus embraced the issues of forced captivity and slavery and yet transcended them. Isaiah's prophecy concerning the opening of prisons and the release of slaves around the year 500 B.C. did not concern him. He did not stay with the picture of what may have been a national rejoicing over the end of the Babylonian captivity. He did not merely proclaim the ancient "year of the Lord's favor," that is, the Year of Jubilees. Jesus used this passage to set forth a universal concept of spiritual liberty affecting every form of bondage and oppression upon mankind in every age. "Today," he told the Nazarenes, "this scripture has been fulfilled in your hearing."[6] That which Isaiah had predicted, he brought in himself.

In the same manner when Jesus told his contemporaries,

"You shall know the truth, and the truth shall make you free,"[7] he was not dealing with such issues as academic freedom in the twentieth century, even though many academic institutions of the day have made these words their motto. Rather Jesus established a basis for spiritual truth, namely, his own; and for spiritual freedom, which was his gift to his followers.

The freedom Jesus proclaimed was freedom from sin. He sought to deliver men from bondage to self, and to rid them of the things that imprison the human spirit—legalism, idolatry, superstition, lust, pride. The same high tone is carried throughout the New Testament. The Apostle Paul wrote, "Where the Spirit of the Lord is, there is liberty."[8] The Apostle James spoke of a "law of liberty" by which Christians were to act.[9] The Apostle Peter urged his hearers to "live as free men, yet without using your freedom as a pretext for evil."[10] This freedom even has eschatological overtones. In the New Testament view, death was a shackling from which the faithful believer would one day be released into the "glorious liberty of the sons of God."[11]

No such theological significance is attached to the kind of freedom symbolized by the Liberty Bell. The signers of the Declaration of Independence spoke reverently of God; they quoted his Word; they ascribed what they called "self-evident truths" to the hand of the Almighty; but their immediate concern was taxation without representation. They demanded political freedom for their constituents in order to achieve economic independence. They said that they were ready to go to war, and if necessary even die, for that kind of freedom.

Today a strong wind of questioning is sweeping through the Western world. Younger thinkers are asking for a re-evaluation of the importance of human freedom. Is it so essential to life and the pursuit of happiness? Are not other things more important—bread and shelter, for instance? A young clergyman from Australia who had just been visiting in Prague remarked to the author, "We have tried for centuries to get economic liberty from political liberty, and we have not made it yet. Perhaps now we should try it the other way around and see how it goes." He was prepared to put his civil liberties into storage for the time being, if it meant the establishment of a social order that would prove more just and beneficial to more people.

Such thinking seems to betray the traditional convictions of most English-speaking citizens. Yet it is becoming increasingly popular every day, and threatens to render obsolete the books that have been written about the spiritual roots of democracy. A few years ago it was all so different. One has only to go back to World War II in America to find a familiar and comfortable atmosphere. Legends of George Washington at Valley Forge, the patriotic writings of Jefferson and Paine, the orations of Patrick Henry and Elbert Hubbard, the various gems of Americana—"Barbara Frietchie," *The Man Without a Country,* "The Stars and Stripes Forever," and trips to the national shrines were all part of it. Words such as "freedom" and "democracy" evoked the strongest passions in the human breast—and still do for millions of people. Joe Rosenthal's photograph of five Marines raising the flag on Mount Suribachi at Iwo Jima captured what seemed the high moment of the war, and was made into a national statue.

Then came the rumblings of disillusionment. As the postwar breakthrough in communications brought the world into one room, it became increasingly evident that great blocks of people in the so-called free world did not really enjoy freedom at all. The faults and failures of Western society showed up like cracks in the walls. One of the five Marines photographed by Rosenthal died an alcoholic, a member of a minority group and a victim of lifelong discrimination. The oncoming generation became vocally critical. It began asking questions about the military necessity that caused the atomic detonations over Hiroshima and Nagasaki. It asked why such a high premium was being placed on human liberty when it was obviously such a partial achievement. It asked whether the staples for survival were not more important than a voting franchise. And to make its questions more embarrassing, it began its own examination of history without the familiar accompaniment of martial music.

As a result, the 1960's began to produce history like the following passage, taken from the work of a prominent American Negro scholar:

The abiding virtues of the "Plymouth gentlemen" and the conservative Puritan colonists of Massachusetts Bay were their strong sense of justice and order, ethics and theology, embedded in the covenants for select whites. . . . This spirit is unmistakable in the colonial state churches where indentured servants and poor whites were segregated by class status to the back pews or standing room in the rear. The freedom Puritans sought and maintained was strictly for themselves and their way of life. . . . Puritans differed from the Israelites in making no provisions in legislation or religious practices to include concern for African slaves or Indians. . . . Consequently the "new Israel" differed from the "old Israel" not in its acceptance of slavery, but in limiting slavery to Africans and linking slavery and being African to human inferiority, decadence, depravity, and degradation. . . . What is difficult to comprehend is why the Puritans alone developed an ineradicable anti-blackness. . . . To the Puritans Africans were nothing.[12]

In the face of such contemporary writing, and in a day when national flags are being burned by serious young demonstrators in the downtown streets of cities, the evangelical Christian is being forced to reestablish—if he can—the spiritual meaning of freedom. Five questions present themselves:

1.What is the relationship of the teaching of the Bible to a democratic form of government?

2. Was the Puritan revolution a genuine liberation of the human spirit, or was it intended to free only Christians of a certain type?

3. Does the Biblical emphasis on the individual soul's value warrant a defense of individual freedom in an age like ours?

4. What are the precise Christian values in such political instruments as the multiparty system, the jury trial, freedom of speech, and religious liberty?

5. Can the New Testament ethic be legitimately applied to a world that refuses the authority of Jesus Christ?

1. The relationship of the Bible's teaching to modern democratic institutions is direct and simple. The issue involved is neither spiritual freedom nor social evolution nor the sacralizing of the profane. Democracy is founded, as evangelical thinkers believe, on the conviction that man is a sinner. It draws its pragmatic strength from the reality of the human condition. In the words of Elton Trueblood, "Democracy is necessitated by the fact that all men are sinners; it is made possible by the fact that we know it."[13] Such thinking underscores the warning of one of democracy's chief architects, President James Madison, who wrote, "The truth is that all men having power ought to be distrusted."[14] Madison learned his doctrine of man as sinner from Dr. Witherspoon at the College of New Jersey. Madison's concept of checks and balances, written into the American Constitution, was designed to prevent any one group of men in any branch of the Federal Government from gaining too much power. In this aim he was backed by John Adams, the second President of the United States, a deist who thought like a Puritan. Said Adams, "The fundamental article of my political creed is that despotism, or unlimited sovereignty, or absolute power,

is the same in a majority of a popular assembly, an aristocratic council, an oligarchical junta, and a single emperor."[15] He was also supported, a few decades later, by John Stuart Mill: "Men, as well as women, do not need political rights in order that they may govern, but in order that they may not be misgoverned."[16]

Not every evangelical has pushed the origins of democracy back to the simple truth that sinners are equal before God. Douglas Campbell, a leading exponent of Puritanism, worked out a more elaborate formulation: "The meanest peasant, once called of God, felt within him a strength stronger than the might of kings. In that mighty elevation of the masses embodied in the Calvinistic doctrines of election and grace, lay the germs of the modern principles of human equality."[17] It is certainly true in Christian experience that the more time a man spends in the courts of his God, the less awe he is likely to feel in the presence of men. How far such an attitude reflects the Puritan or Calvinist mind as a whole, it is impossible to tell. There is stronger support, perhaps, for the view that attributes the roots of democracy not so much to good will or exalted feelings as to a realistic facing of the sinfulness and untrustworthiness of man.

C. S. Lewis has said,

I believe in political equality. But there are two opposite reasons for being a democrat. You may think all men so good that they deserve a share in the government of the commonwealth, and so wise that the commonwealth needs their advice. That is, in my opinion, the false, romantic doctrine of democracy. On the other hand, you may believe fallen men to be so wicked that not one of them can be trusted with any irresponsible power over his fellows. That I believe to be the true ground of democracy. . . . Since we have learned sin, we have found, as Lord Acton says, that "all power corrupts, and absolute power corrupts absolutely." The only remedy has been to take away the powers and substitute a legal fiction of equality. . . . Theocracy has been rightly abolished not because it is bad that learned priests should govern ignorant laymen, but because priests are wicked men like the rest of us. . . . As St. Paul writes, to have died for valuable men would have been not divine but merely heroic; but God died for sinners. He loved us not because we were lovable, but because he is Love. . . . If there is equality it is in his love, not in us.[18]

Not every evangelical would agree perhaps with Lewis' description of equality as a "legal fiction," for Paul makes it clear in many Scripture passages that the differences between men are indistinguishable at the cross. That there is no gradation among sinners, and that (as Lewis says) God loves us all equally, is not fiction but truth.

2. The question of the spiritual value of the Puritan revolt is submerged in the 1960's in the total question of the value of Christianity at all. If there is one impression that the visitor to Europe gains today, it is that Europe is tired of religion. The modern Continental is weary of hearing about the bigoted priests, preachers, monks, elders, and congregations of the past. Where Protestants once complained about Roman Catholic persecution, and Romans berated Protestant intolerance, today's generation is sick of both. No point is served therefore by a fresh effort to salvage either Calvinism or Puritanism. There have been too many burnings, hangings, torturings, cart-tail whippings, witch-hunts, and similar demonstrations of inhumanity perpetrated in the name of Jesus of Nazareth. The record of what Calvin did to Servetus, what Cromwell did to the Irish at Drogheda, and what the Massachusetts Bay Colony ministers did to innocent people at Salem, stands under divine judgment along with the St. Bartholomew's Day massacre. No partisan pleading can wipe out the stain of cruelty. The moving finger, having writ, moves on.

These dreadful acts, however, must not be allowed to

obscure the historical record, lest another wrong be committed. The truth is that at the very time when the Puritans were allowing their zeal to slip its bounds, they were winning one of the most important political victories in the history of man. The battle was joined not on a military plain or upon the high seas, but in the lower house of the British Parliament. Ever since Magna Carta the English people had been developing a rugged spirit of independence and a love of liberty. The Tudor dynasty, with the brief exception of the boy king Edward VI, did everything it could to stifle such a spirit in the body politic. During the sixteenth century the winds coming off the Continent stirred the aspirations of the island folk afresh. It became impossible to separate the desire to reform the Church of England from a move to check the political powers of an autocratic monarch.

When the Roman Catholic sovereign Mary Tudor succeeded to the English throne in 1553, a large number of evangelical churchmen fled to the Continent. Hundreds of them gathered at Geneva, where John Calvin was expounding the Scriptures. During their stay they edited and published an English Bible known as the "Geneva Bible." It was forbidden in England because in the marginal notes it said some incendiary things about the Christian's duty to resist tyrannical rulers in the name of God. Upon the ascension of Elizabeth, Mary's Protestant half-sister, in 1558, some eight hundred of the exiles returned to England and Scotland, where they began encouraging independent thought. Hopefully they dreamed of revolutionary changes in church and state. They set out to test the new queen. When they were arrested, they protested in the name of religious liberty. The rights of the individual were set against the royal prerogative. Elizabeth proved unyielding; as head of church and state she insisted upon a policy of religious uniformity, and so set the stage for the next act. That was the Puritan exodus to the

New World and the Puritan overthrow of the monarchy.

During the first half of the seventeenth century the Puritans fought and won a titanic battle for political freedom in Britain. The power of the Stuart kings was permanently broken by a handful of lawmakers sitting in London. Their brilliance, conviction, and courage have perhaps never been matched in the history of elected assemblies. Today most of the free traditions existing under Commonwealth and American law, as well as legal rights in many independent nations, hark back to the years 1620-1640 when tremendous issues for man were being debated at Westminster on the bank of the Thames. No one today recalls the names of Sir Edward Coke, Sir John Eliot, John Pym, and John Hampden. They have been honorably retired into the annals of history. Yet it was these men and their colleagues who used English law to take absolute power away from a furious and dreaded monarch. They gave their electorate—*for the first time in recorded history*—the right to govern itself through its representatives chosen in free and open election.

Was the Puritan revolution an emancipation of the human spirit? Such a view could not have been formed at Pride's Purge, or at the trial of Anne Hutchinson. The famous "blue laws," it is now known, never existed; yet there were many unpleasant aspects to Puritan dogmatism. By contrast, the Puritans unquestionably bequeathed political freedom to the world and did it deliberately. In theory at least that freedom was not restricted to a particular church, nation, or race. Thomas Hooker, in his famous sermon to the Connecticut General Court in 1638, declared,

The choice of public magistrates belongs unto the people by God's own allowance . . . because the foundation of authority is laid, firstly, in the free consent of the people. By a free choice, the hearts of the people will be more inclined to the love of the persons [chosen] and more ready to yield [obedience]. The privilege of election, which belongs to the people, must be exercised according to the blessed will and law of God. . . . The lesson is taught that as God hath spared our lives, and given them in liberty, so to seek the guidance of God, and to choose in God and for God. The lesson is taught to persuade us, as God hath given us liberty, to *take* it.[19]

There it is. No royal charter; no concession from some existing state; no select covenant for the "white saints." Rather it is government of the people, by the people, and for the people. "It is on the banks of the Connecticut, under the mighty preaching of Thomas Hooker, and in the constitution to which he gave life, if not form, we draw the first breath of that atmosphere which is now so familiar to us."[20]

3. The evangelical Christian is traditionally a defender of the rights of the individual. Today those rights have been challenged and restricted by a multiplex society until many are seriously questioning whether any one single person really has any rights at all. The evangelical insists on the importance of individual men and women on the ground of Scripture, and particularly because of the incarnation of God in Jesus Christ. "The enthronement . . . of the individual . . . rested upon a religious idea which was this—that as an incarnate God, while wearing our flesh, had once died for every man, so no man thus redeemed could, without sacrilege, be abased by any tyranny of prelate or king from his privilege of remaining 'a child of God and an inheritor of the kingdom of heaven.' "[21]

The Apostle Paul minimized his individuality only to emphasize the power of the Spirit of God to indwell that individuality: "I have been crucified with Christ, it is no longer I who live, but Christ who lives in me. . . ."[22] The Christian's identity is that of a person both inner-directed (by the Holy Spirit) and other-directed (by the teaching of

Scripture). But the indwelling occurs in *me,* rather than in *us.* As Lord MacLeod has said, "The only ultimate reason why man as man has individual significance is because Christ died for him."[23] Helmut Thielicke echoes: "Man becomes a holy thing, a neighbor, only if we realize that he is the property of God and that Jesus Christ died for him."[24]

The logic of the New Testament emphasis seems to be that unless something happens to *me,* it will not happen to *us.* The *individual* must be imbued by the holy desire; *he* must be kindled by the flame of God; *he* must be accepted in the Beloved; *he* must become God's messenger to the world—or nothing takes place. The man is not the church so much as the church is the man. The Protestant Reformation, the Puritan revolt, the evangelical awakening, all became movements because individual men and women turned to the Bible and read it for themselves. Thanks to the labors of Renaissance scholarship they could read it in their own language, without Jerome's latinisms or emendations by the Holy See. As a result, they made history.

Today mankind is being forced to learn another lesson: in an interlocking society, individualism is not enough. Men are still born alone, they still die alone, and they still come to Jesus Christ alone; but the modern world is forcing them to live most of their waking moments together. Interdependence has supplanted independence as the rule of life. The evangelical's social conscience requires that he play his part as a member of the team of humanity. If there is poverty, he should be taking a lead in seeking to eradicate it. If there is injustice, he should be an Amos, pointing it out. If there is corruption, he should be helping to turn the rascals out. If there is waste, he should be acting the role of the good steward.

It is in this role, rather than in the stance of the pristine rugged individualist, that the evangelical Christian can make his best contribution. The eternal store he sets by each human soul will become more evident as he makes his witness to the largest possible number. He will not use his freedom to work against his neighbor's good.[25] Instead of championing the individual *against* the group or the mass, he will be safeguarding the accessibility of the individual *within* the group or mass to the claims of Christ and to the benefits of society as a whole.

4. An extremely subtle relationship exists between the teaching of the Bible and the free instruments of a democracy, such as a free press, a multiparty system, the right of an accused person to be considered innocent until he is proved guilty, habeas corpus, and freedom of religion. Many think there is no relationship, and they quote chapter and verse to "prove" it. The evangelical believes there is a connection, and he turns for support to the Communist governments.

There are few living in the West who would care to make a case for freedom of religion in Communist countries, whether in the Sino- or Soviet bloc. In a Communist election only one party ever prepares a slate of candidates. A free press is unheard of; so is free speech; so is a writ of habeas corpus. As for the presumed innocence of prisoners, a Communist cadre in China put it graphically: "There is no need in our society for prisoners to be protected by the presumption of innocence. Our socialist officials never make a mistake. When we arrest you, you are guilty. It is only in decadent Western cultures, where they have corrupt bourgeois officials, that prisoners need such protection."[26]

It is not coincidental, the evangelical believes, that the Bible is virtually forbidden in such countries. Queen Elizabeth I prohibited the Geneva Bible from coming into Britain for the same reason: the Word of God stirs men. It forces them to think; it creates dissatisfaction with totalitarian systems. The Bible gives men an appetite for freedom and justice. It causes them to stretch themselves to their full height and to demand their inheritance as made in the divine image. It is when countries that have had the heritage of an open Bible are compared with those without such a tradition that the healthy relationship of evangelical Christianity to justice in the social order is best seen.

5. The final question—Can the New Testament ethic be legitimately applied to a world that refuses the authority of Jesus Christ?—belongs to the chapters that follow.

Chapter 9

God Made a Colorful World

*The poorest Boys and Girls within this Province, such as are
of the lowest condition, whether they be Indians or English
or Ethiopians—they have the same Right to Religion and Life
that the Richest Heirs have. And they who go about to deprive
them of this Right, they attempt the bombarding of Heaven;
and the shells they throw shall fall down upon their own heads.*

—Judge Samuel Sewall of Boston, Massachusetts, "to Addington
Davenport, Esq., going to Judge Smith of Sandwich
for killing his Negro, 1719."

Since God is for man in Christ Jesus, the evangelical holds
that God is for all men everywhere. No matter what *men* may
think of other men, *God* is for them. His primordial thoughts
toward man are for good and not for evil. He would "have
all men to be saved and to come to the knowledge of the
truth."[1] To that end he sent his Son, the Lord Jesus Christ,
to pay a price for men of every race and color. On the cross
outside Jerusalem no favorites were played. To quote a man
from Tarsus, in God's sight there is no difference among
men.[2] All have sinned, all have come under condemnation.[3]
But at the same time, every man has equal approach to the
benefits of Christ's atonement.[4]

So clear is the Bible's teaching at this point that it is hard
to account for the ways in which men have deliberately read

their own prejudices into the text. It took 1,400 years to com-
pile the sixty-six books of the Old and New Testaments, yet
nowhere in them is a person considered inferior because of
his race or color. The religious arguments of the past which
have been used to foster unjust and unhealthy racial attitudes
were based upon an un-Biblical theology and an incorrect
exegesis of Scripture. Men have tried in other years, and they
will try again to fit God into their molds, but it will not
work. The good Lord indulges no favorite colors. He loves
us all because he made us all.

The physical appearance of man is an aspect of his life
that concerns God least.[5] Today people do not even know
what his Son looked like; the only thing certain is that he was
not the "fair god" of red hair and blue eyes that so many
artists have tried to make him. To be an evangelical Christian in the 1960's is to be color-blind as Jesus was. It is to
look with eyes of compassion upon every human being,
counting each to be of ultimate worth in God's sight no
matter what his spiritual needs. The Christian view does not
minimize racial traits or group characteristics; these distinctions are part of the infinite variety with which God has en-
riched our colorful world.

Different patterns of skin pigmentation have developed
among men, but they provide no rationale for segregation
today on our shrinking planet. It is a mark of original sin
that men take their greatest pride in things over which they
exercise no control and for which they can take absolutely
no credit. Human skin color falls into this category. As
Billy Graham has said, skin color does not matter to God
because he is looking upon the heart.[6] The evangelical Christian of the new generation wants to apply the Biblical standard to bring social justice to racial minority groups. He does
not have to be reminded that there are demonstrable in-
equalities among men, but he insists on going back to the

premise that men have equal standing in the eyes of him who created them. The evangelical wants that equality built into the laws that govern men.

Not only does the Bible fail to support a doctrine of inherent racial superiority; none of the sciences, whether anthropology, sociology, psychology, archaeology, or any related field of research, will yield a basis for such belief. If it be argued that some races are historically backward, science points to the causes: lack of access to raw materials, geographic isolation, poor cross-fertilization of ideas, inbreeding, ravages of disease, tribal warfare, and so forth. There is simply no way for the racist to get off the hook; he is up against too much evidence. If he wants to get along here and in Heaven, he is going to have to join the human race. There is segregation in hell, but he will not like it.

The new evangelical is weary of the subterfuges used to justify the preferential treatment of one race over another. He finds it incredible that anyone—Christian or non-Christian—should judge himself to be superior to another person on the basis of racial origin. He belongs to a fresh day in which man-made, artificial attempts to cleave the unity of the human race will not hold. "God made all men of one," said the Apostle Paul.[7] So be it. Beneath all the diversity, the Bible posits a fundamental unity based not on the similarity of species but on a more significant element: the fact of human sin and the accessibility of God's Grace.

Seen from the perspective of Scripture, any movement that seeks to eliminate racial injustice among men, and at the same time to avoid perpetrating a fresh injustice, is in the favor of God. Any lawful effort to redress social grievances caused by unfair discrimination among men is according to the mind of Christ. But so devious are the wiles of Satan, and so complex the intricacies of human sin, that the righting of an ancient wrong can inflict new, unfair hardships upon the descendants of those who created the original wrong. This injustice in turn fosters anxiety and dread which form the precondition of sin.

As the nations talk peace and prepare for racial war, anxiety hovers over the whole world. Christians have no magic string to lead the way out of the maze. Who is wise enough to judge between Jew and Arab, Greek and Turk, Indian and Pakistani, or between any other parties to ethnic or linguistic quarrels? Who has the formula that will bring peace with justice in Vietnam, or Korea, or Berlin? But the evangelical believes that what hate and revenge and pride cannot do, love can. Love is the human face of social justice. Love alone, without skill, will not make a good law, but love will provide the basis of moral authority that will make a good law work. It is the one great balm for the endless hostilities besetting the races of mankind. It is the one hope for the world's trouble spots.

The world has rarely accepted the law of love as a basis for human relationships; the evangelical does so, but is tempted to limit his thinking to clichés and generalities. He is beginning to realize that this is no longer possible; he is faced with direct social responsibility. If love is the answer, love is something you do. It cannot be created by the enactment of statutes requiring men to display comradeship toward each other. No such statute has been promulgated in the history of humanity. The law will not even guarantee that men accord each other decent treatment. The law can set bounds, it cannot set an example. To illustrate: the passage of civil rights laws in America has given the Negro citizen greatly needed help in recent years by clarifying his status and giving him fuller possession of his birthright. Yet the civil rights laws have not increased in the slightest the respect and affection between men of the white and Negro races; and these very qualities are supremely needed to ease the existing tensions. Experts in race relations are surprised to find tensions in parts of America worsening rather than lessening. The Christian is not surprised, for he knows what the law can and cannot do. A sociologist was astonished to find that after teaching a course on race prejudice, some of his students were more prejudiced at the end than at the beginning. The Christian is not astonished, for he is convinced that the answer is not education alone.

If love is the answer to the racial confusion of our day, then how is love created? The Apostle Paul describes it as a "fruit of the Spirit."[8] John explains, "We love because he first loved us."[9] Love is basically a positive response to a prior love. Love is created when the Spirit of God takes over a human life to incarnate the teaching of divine truth. Words of persuasion and instruction are backed by deeds of affection and sacrifice, all motivated by a higher source of good.

Here is a supreme opportunity for the evangelical Christian in our time. The world is perishing for the saving love of God, actualized in practical situations by persons of ultimate worth. The evangelical is active in a church where persons can be saved and set free to love all men. He could find no better place of service; yet in candor he must admit that the church is among the most carved-up, segregated institutions in the free world. It has failed to take Jesus' command of love seriously, and has listened to lamentable advice on the subject of the superficial differences between groups of people. Evangelical Christians have much ground to recover in the field of race relations. The world is forcing them to admit that their efforts to cross land and sea to make converts to Christ have not always been accompanied by wisdom. Too often they have shamefully neglected the very conditions at home that they were so zealous to correct on the mission field.

Some of the ablest missionaries, furthermore, have taken

with them to foreign fields a secret contempt for the "natives" that is now backfiring upon the whole church. The new evangelical generation is being challenged to rectify the situation by assuming the lead in the task of reconciliation. People of other continents will continue to hold the white man's sins against him, but there is one weapon that they cannot resist. That is a genuine, sincere, unaffected love for people regardless of race, color, or religion, and that is the supreme gift of Jesus Christ our Lord. Those who love Christ have a moral responsibility to work at the business of racial friendship and racial justice, on and off the job, at every waking hour.

For example, the disciple of Jesus is required to ask daily in self-examination whether his own social conscience reflects the Mind and Spirit of his Master. Is he really facing up to the implications of the Parable of the Last Judgment?[10] Does he really care what happens to his unfortunate brother? And if he does care, will he say or do anything about it when the opportunity arises; that is to say, when the pressure is on? Is he presently engaged in a sincere effort to obtain justice and equity for those less favored in the fields of education, housing, job opportunity, and health and medical services? Or is he content to make noises in his throat and turn to the sport pages of the newspaper? In God's Master Plan of the universe there is space for neither embittered integration nor righteous segregation. God's Word makes it clear that at the point of human relations the endowing Creator will not be satisfied with token justice. He want hearts melted and lives set free to serve him.

Today's evangelical is equally dissatisfied with the clichés about race that have been used in the past to salve religious people's consciences. One of the commonest repeats the point that has just been made: "Laws will not work, but a change of heart will." The trouble is that such phrases can be rolled about on their tongues by people who have not the slightest intention of ever making a gesture to ease the lot of another race which history has placed in their midst in an unfavorable social position. Under the circumstances such expressions can be pretty dreadful. Man's capacity for self-deception is always greater than he thinks it is. That is why love often requires a law with teeth in it.

Two personal experiences are introduced at this point for illustrative purposes. The writer attended a meeting in Seattle, Washington in 1948, at which the speaker was a nationally known Bible teacher. He was addressing a group of University of Washington students in a campus church. When the question period arrived, he was asked for his views on the race question. The man responded generously and at great length, offering a complete exposition of Ephesians 2, which he said demonstrated beyond doubt that God had demolished all "walls of partition" between the various races of mankind. In the Father's sight, said he, there are no distinctions whatever, thanks to the work of Jesus Christ on the cross. Then he added, "As to the question of a Negro and a white minister being allowed to use the same bathroom at a Bible conference, I would say that was a matter of no consequence."

With unerring instinct the Bible teacher touched upon the exact point where his teaching became relevant—and flunked. His interpretation of Ephesians did not insist upon equal privileges in the public toilet. Love—Christian love—will not fuss about plumbing. Love is a principle that works. It is a flag that flies a welcome to every potential fellow believer, and that, of course, leaves out nobody. It is more than glad to underscore the welcome by setting up ground rules that insure basic justice.

In 1966 while flying over the Atlantic ocean by jet, the writer found his seatmate to be a prominent Dutch industrialist. During the conversation the Dutchman asked for the writer's views on the race problem in the South, and "what we intended to do about it." An hour later the discussion had switched to World War II, and he remarked that he had spent four years during the war in the underground. What did he think of the Germans? "I hate them," he said, "and I shall hate them till I die." But did he not believe there were many exeellent German people? "I'll tell you what the trouble with Europe is," he retorted. "There are about seventy million too many people in it. And they're all Germans." This man spied out the mote of racial unrest in America's eye, but could not get the German beam out of his own eye. No doubt many share his feelings. When Christ floods the heart with his love, such hostilities are dissolved by the divine chemistry. Until then they must be contained by law.

What is needed is a baptism of love that refuses to consider any man an enemy, but selects as primary target the victim of racial discrimination and injustice. To implement such a thrust, however, the evangelical is forced to recognize that he is just emerging from the "Rip van Winkle period" of his social history, during which his racial attitudes, particularly toward the Negro, were affected by a drowsy and careless social conscience. The Civil War split the great evangelical denominations but left the Negro out of both sides. Despite the intensive efforts of certain groups such as the Quakers, no broad-gauge concern was felt throughout the evangelical Christian community to implement the American promise of "equal justice under law." Lynchings created shock but little more. The New Testament's inspired approach to the race problem was ignored. When the waves of poor immigrants arrived from Europe and the Orient, the reaction of Anglo-Saxon Protestants was often strong disapproval. Southern and eastern Europeans, along with Chinese, Filipinos, American Indians, Japanese, Mexicans, Negroes, and Jews, were kept out of "the better part of town." So the downtrodden remained downtrodden, while the sons of those who came to America early to escape religious persecution grew affluent on the cheap labor available. A flintlike resistance was presented to the radical social challenge of the Gospel. To palliate feelings, many an orthodox congregation established a mission in the foreign ghetto across the tracks; and once a year the poor folk of darker complexion got to come and sit in the big oak pews. Segregation became a comfortable habit, the pulpit was muffled, and the social concern of the churchgoer was tragically frozen.

Today the evangelical finds it incredible that such a condition should ever have existed in the church of Jesus Christ. He is scandalized to read that fifty years ago Christian people were still turning out such songs as "Lil pickaninny kid, de Lawd gwine make you white someday." He is relieved and heartened to discover in the Bible, and here and there in church history, evidences that there have always been those among God's people who were able to transcend differences of race and color. Even the vexing question of intermarriage seems to have been dealt with in Scripture.[11] Evangelicals are coming to believe that there is nothing in the New Testament to indicate that believers are not free to marry in the faith whom they choose.

The moral solution to the race issue lies within the framework of the Word of God. As stewards of the mysteries of Grace, today's evangelicals bear the message of reconciliation that the world is longing to hear. They know the word from beyond: "If the Son therefore shall make you free, ye shall be free indeed."[12]

Three cautionary words need to be added at this point. First, it is not necessarily this chapter's intent to show that more evangelicals should be participating in sit-ins, wade-ins, pray-ins, demonstrations, and acts of civil disobedience.

Demonstrations differ in quality. For example, a number of Charles G. Finney's Oberlin professors were once jailed for rescuing a captured runaway slave from the hands of a United States marshal. Few people today would have sympathized with the marshal's desire to perpetuate slavery. Yet there are among contemporary religious leaders those who have come close to making an idol of the race issue. They seem to insist that a man cannot become a Christian unless his racial attitudes are satisfactory; that salvation is in fact not free but has a price tag on it; that Jesus does not bid a man come to him just as he is, sin and all, without one plea, but that he first has to sign some kind of pledge.

The Gospel of Jesus Christ is not cheap and it is not costly; it is absolutely free to sinners. The repentant one soon learns that he is to obey God's words to Isaiah: "Cease to do evil; learn to do good."[13] He soon learns that he is to take the yoke of Christ and learn of him; that he is to unlock his heart and love all men, including those he hated. But the first word of the Gospel is not "Sign the pledge," the first word is "Come!" The first word is, "My blood was shed for you." The first word is, "Ho, everyone that thirsteth, come to the waters and buy, without money and without price."[14] Take that word away from the Gospel, and it becomes another gospel.

Second, the evangelical will find the above expression of caution no loophole. He has not thereby been excused from the struggle for human justice or racial justice. He has become, by the Grace of God, a person of ultimate worth; he has been redeemed and liberated by the atoning death of Christ; he has been turned loose to be a benediction to society all his days. If he does not join the Negro marches, he had better make sure that it is because he has found a more effective way to contribute to the racial struggle—by working for the peaceful integration of a neighborhood, school, or church; by remedial teaching; by practical, self-giving love in specific situations.

Third, the fact that God loves us all includes the fact that he loves the white man in the American South and the Afrikaner in South Africa. Too many workers for racial justice are filled with hate for these people; they are, in their zeal for righteousness, ready to consign them all to a kind of secularized hell. God is not so willing. He loves them. He is calling them on the same terms he calls the civil rights workers. He wants to make them his own and to implant in them his Gospel of love for all men.

One of the most moving testimonies in years to the influence of Jesus Christ was given by a 75-year-old Negro citizen, Mr. James Emory Bond, over station WBAL-TV in Baltimore, Maryland on February 4, 1964. Walking into the television studio without an appointment, Mr. Bond offered his views on a civic problem. He was interviewed unrehearsed for an hour and a half, and said among other things,

When the Gospel hit me I hated white people. I had sat at the feet of ex-slaves. I had sat at the feet of veterans of the Civil War with legs cut off and arms off and so on—maimed. I sat there and they told me of the atrocities that were wrought upon them when they were slaves, which we don't read in the books. They told those things. I remember the white folks down there where we were raised, and the boys throwing stones at me when I walked up the road to go to my little hut back in the woods to get a little learning. And my father told me to fight it and not take it. And I grew up with that in me.

I heard the Gospel at twenty-five years and six months old. I sat down and listened to the preacher preach the Gospel. [The evangelist was Billy Sunday.] And when the preacher preached the Gospel, and I stepped up according to the custom, it came over me—and I've loved white men ever since. Loved them ever since! My hate turned into love and never changed even from that day to today. That's what it did to me. It changed me from a rascal and a fool to somebody that loved people and can think about these things.[15]

Such is the testimony of the heart of one man to the good news of Jesus Christ. If it seems strange, the reason is that a different set of principles is in operation. James Emory Bond discovered the meaning of God's forgiveness, and implemented in practice what many evangelicals are beginning to do in new and significant ways. At long last the Spirit of God seems to be finding servants eager to heal one of the worst sores to plague men on earth.

Chapter 10

Right Versus Wrong

I'm tired, tired of puppets instead of people,
Of persons who drop soliloquies carefully labeled intelligence.
I'm tired of cynics who call themselves realists,
Tired of minds rotting in indifference,
Of people bored because they're afraid to care;
I'm tired of people who have to be entertained,
Of girls proud of knowing the score and snickering about it;
I'm tired of sophisticated slobs,
Tired of people with nothing better to do than glue their days
*   together with alcohol.*
I'm tired of people embarrassed at honesty, at love, at knowledge.
Tired, yes . . . very tired.

—Submitted by a girl student to the newspaper of
Arizona State University, 1964

Morality, the conforming of men to virtuous principles of conduct, is not the exclusive property of the Christian church. Human goodness came into the world by the hand of God with the first man and has never left. Truth, as John A. Mackay says, is in order to goodness; and goodness was here before sin.[1] Further, goodness is social. It is in the nature of a social organism to establish guidelines for the good behavior of its members. The process has brought into being moralists who have sought to distinguish good from evil. All civilizations, including those unconnected with Chris-

91

tianity in any form, have produced moralists in the course of their history. Many have stood tall against their cultural backgrounds; a few have been superb.

Nevertheless in today's Western world down to the 1960's, morality has been considered by many to be the peculiar precinct of Christianity. The churches themselves have looked upon faith and morals as two sides of the same coin. Their theologians have battled for centuries as to whether faith or morals takes priority in God's plan of salvation. The Reformation took the revealed New Testament formula: Man is saved by faith, and faith works out as morality. "As many as received him, to them gave he power to become the sons of God."[2] "We are his workmanship, created in Christ Jesus unto good works."[3] "If we live in the Spirit, let us also walk in the Spirit."[4] But for millions of people the sheer moral force of the Gospel has been its most impressive aspect. To them the words "good" and "Christian" are synonymous.

The church has been a good teacher. It has taught many generations that Christian behavior is built upon personal morality (purity) and social morality (love). It has held a man's body to be the temple of the Holy Spirit. Christians have been enjoined to practice honesty and rectitude in their dealings; to avoid gossip, strife, and the temptations of the flesh. Sometimes this code has been known as chivalry, sometimes as asceticism, sometimes as good works, sometimes as the Puritan conscience, sometimes as character. The name changes, but the influence lasts; and the result has been beneficent to the human race. Had we lived in the first century, we might have met a Cilician tentmaker endeavoring to live by this code. Had we lived in the Dark Ages, it could have been an Arthurian knight; in the twelfth century, a medieval nun; in the sixteenth, an Anabaptist lay preacher. A hundred years ago we might have found a cowboy evangelist in west Texas following the same rules. Today the man next to us in the airplane may well be a member of the Fellowship of Christian Athletes. He, too, would be living after the same manner. It has been a wonderful way of life. Not an easy way, for it has often proved extremely rugged; but a wonderful way nonetheless.

In our day, despite the continued adherence of many to the moral principles of the Bible, a radical transformation is taking place in Western society. People's moral attitudes are changing. The old behavioral concepts are being retooled. Doubt is being cast upon traditional values that have long been considered beyond question. Truth is once again being relegated to what Pilate held it to be: something impossible to discover. At best, many believe, it can only be approximated. Traits such as modesty, decency, marital fidelity, and family loyalty, which have formed the underpinning of so many civilizations, are being reappraised and even stigmatized as tenets of "bourgeois morality." The strongest impetus to this denigration came of course from Karl Marx and his precursors and successors. Josef Stalin declared that "there is no such thing as eternal truth." To call the "new morality" a Communist trick, however, is no longer possible. It has become a strong development within the social establishment itself, fostered by the leaders of Western culture, including officers of the bench and the church.

With the publication of the Kinsey report in 1948, what the world has labeled the "Puritan" attitude toward personal morality moved into its final phase of eclipse.[5] To speak more accurately, the Bible was outmoded as a chief point of reference in the moral confusion. Many churches have continued to survive as conventional social pockets, retaining the post-Victorian appearance of normality. Insulated from the filth mystique, their older members have comported and still comport themselves with the decorum of yesterday, relatively unaware of the paralysis of personal morals that is creeping upon the body politic.

"This moral condition," writes Dean Elmer Homrighausen,

"is expressed in cheating in the academic world, deals in the political world, unscrupulous experimentation in the scientific world, promiscuity and infidelity in the sexual and domestic world. Perhaps the point at which this decadence is most evident is in the area of sex, for sex has become a dominant obsession in American life; indeed, it has been made into an idolatry."[6] Motion pictures, which are a fair barometer of the moral climate, have introduced in recent years a more permissive attitude toward adultery, fornication, nudity, vulgarity, and profanity, as well as greater lenience toward crimes of violence, alcoholism, drug addiction, and personal standards in general. Television, which by virtue of its home consumption is not quite so permissive (except in Britain), has nevertheless wielded even greater influence in creating the moral revolution.

More important than the external criteria of the revolution are its ethical and philosophical presuppositions. For convenience, these may be looked at individually.

1. *The utilitarian ethic.* As taught in most Western universities, this ethic appeals to the scientific mind. It prefers to ask of a thing, not "Is it good?" but rather, "Is it useful?" Goodness either in essence or in relation to persons is considered something impossible to establish, whereas utility value is either present or is not. All duties can thus be subsumed under the single duty of producing utility values.

2. *The ethic of relativism.* What may be esteemed a proper moral standard in a given culture is, by the premises of this ethic, not necessarily a universal principle. Another culture, or perhaps another age, might consider it quite wrong. Thus morality, to quote a Hollywood starlet, becomes a matter of geography. If it be true, as the anthropologists assure us, that some Eskimos lend their wives to the men who stay at home when they leave on a whaling expedition, what (we are asked) happens to the universal concept of marital fidelity?

Justice Arthur G. Klein of the New York State Supreme
Court was making the same point when he said that certain
smut-filled books were not obscene "when examined in the
light of current community standards."[7] The local environment, in other words, cooks up its own rules. Supreme Court
Justice Holmes gave this position status when he said that
the law is whatever the current judges say it is.[8]

3. *The situation ethic.* This pragmatic approach to morality
has been freshly treated by a number of English and American theologians in the past decade. The unique element in its
revival is the emphasis placed upon love. Bishop John Robinson says in *Honest to God* that love is "the only ethic which
offers a point of constancy in a world of flux."[9] Joseph Fletcher
applies the situation ethic by saying that "if a lie is told un-
lovingly it is wrong, evil; if it is told in love it is good, right."
In other words, "Whatever is the most loving thing in the
situation is the right and good thing."[10] The "situationists"
do not discount the value of the experience of the race, or the
teaching of the Bible, or the importance of the law of the
land; but none of these is considered binding. Rather the
conditions themselves, and the individual's own determination to face them in love, will determine what he shall do.

4. *The social ethic.* For a growing number of people in
today's world there really is no other ethic; that is to say,
social ethics have replaced personal ethics. The slogan currently popular among youth around the world, MAKE LOVE,
DON'T MAKE WAR, sets the theme. The interest in humanitarian
issues has shrunk personal sins into "peccadilloes." If two
people decide to use each other's bodies for purposes of personal gratification, that is held to be their own business providing they are consenting adults. Social problems such as
the rights of minority groups, the care of retarded children,
the fight against cancer, the control of nuclear weapons—these
are now called the essence of true morality. War, and the

right to wage it, is of course the paramount issue. The social ethic places a maximum value on survival. Life itself is held to be the supreme good. If a person embraces enlightened views about society as a whole, he is considered moral, and as a rule no further questions are asked.

5. *The naturalistic ethic.* This hardy perennial has been blooming since the days of Lucretius, and exercises a powerful influence in any age, including our own. By its terms the natural thing is the proper and right thing to do; in the words of Alexander Pope, "Whatever is, is right." The combined effects of the writings of Darwin and Freud may be said to have buttressed this position in the popular mind by eliminating the soul of man in favor of his animal nature. A modern variant of this view is something called "the ethic of the esthetic."

6. *The existential ethic.* As expounded by Jean-Paul Sartre, this ethic simply makes a case for one's duty to humanity in the face of a completely meaningless universe. It is the ethic of Immanuel Kant brought up to date, sans the "starry heavens above."[11]

The one element common to all these positions is their opposition to the *theological ethic* which is based on the given Word of God in the Bible. The Biblical position is variously attacked as legalistic, as wooden, as unloving, as biased. The evangelical university student, taught on Sunday that the Bible's position on morality is the position of God himself, finds himself in a class on Monday in which the whole ethical structure of traditional Christianity is jettisoned as unworkable. He reads his campus newspaper and learns that personal morals are considered by the "new left" to be as out of date as Ussher's chronology. The whole question of Biblical authority becomes a crucial one for him. Precisely what is the relation of Scripture to the changing ethical climate? Is it one of outright condemnation, or is there something to be said to justify what is taking place?

Certainly it can be said that there are absolutes in the Bible that permit no deviation. Faith is always better than doubt; courage is always better than fear (if we except the fear of God); love is always better than hate; hope is always better than despair. God considers theft to be theft, rape to be rape, murder to be murder. Goodness will be praised, evil will be judged. The ethics of relativism, naturalism, and existentialism are rejected because they accept no fixed principle of goodness and they posit no Supreme Being.

> In vain we call old notions fudge,
>   And bend our conscience to our dealing;
> The Ten Commandments will not budge
>   And stealing will continue stealing.[12]

So far, so good. What about the other emerging ethical systems—utilitarian, situational, social? There is work to be done in these fields by evangelical thinkers, and it is long past due. For example, does the Bible ever commend a thing as "good" because it is "useful"? What about the action of Rahab the harlot?[13] What about Jesus' Parable of the Unjust Steward?[14] The issue is acute, for the utilitarian ethic is being employed for immense profit by peddlers of the "playboy" philosophy of sex, and the results are, by almost any standard, injurious to the human race. According to this philosophy, women are accessories to be used, much as in primitive times, rather than persons to be esteemed and loved. Commercial interests are hiring lawyers to defend pornography in the courts and are claiming that obscenity is a useful "necessity" for mankind. Evangelicals are astonished to find a crusade for what they consider rampant evil to be going on in their midst, but they have not moved beyond the point of indignation to separate the true from the false in the utilitarian ethic.

Few significant voices are opposing the "new morality." Most people simply shrug their shoulders—until their children become involved. "The present moral deterioration," writes Dean Homrighausen, "is not a temporary relaxation of standards; rather it is unique, because for many people the past is dead and the objective distinction between good and evil is unclear and even questionable. Moral relativism breeds a flabby conscience. For many moralists, the root of our moral condition is the decline of a meaningful belief in God and of a reverence for the holy at the center of life."[15] Significantly, the *Christian Century* has declared itself in support of "an increasing number of Americans who find wanton public descriptions of man's sexual nature and behavior repugnant and dangerous and who demand that the courts legally restrict such expressions." It says such people are "angered by the ease with which young people in major cities can purchase photographs which depict male and female genitals in exaggerated and titillating postures, and magazines and books which describe in minute and lurid detail every form of hetero- and homosexual aberration and which encourage the expression of latent sadism and masochism in sexual relations." It adds that "many responsible, intelligent . . . people are genuinely disturbed by . . . the increasing number of panderers who for selfish purposes cultivate this craving and by the panderers' concentration of their sales campaign on youth."[16]

There is no doubt that God intended goodness to have a utility value. That is a far cry from saying that usefulness has replaced goodness as an ethic. Certain Nazi extremists found Jewish skin useful for making lampshades—

Again, the concept of love as the basis of "situation ethics" is one that needs thorough investigation by evangelical thought. When the "situationists" say that love is the only sure guide to ethical decisions, the question needs to be asked, "What kind of love?" The Scripture has a high view of love. It tells us that God is love; that it was his love for men that sent his Son to the cross. The Apostle Paul writes that neither wisdom nor generosity nor martyrdom itself has any meaning apart from love.[17] But would Paul have said, "We are willing to follow principles and precepts *if* they serve love, *when* they do"? Would he have threatened, "Neither the state nor its laws are boss for the situationist"?[18] Would he not rather have pointed out that the law itself is an expression of love, of people seeking to distribute justice among all men?

Professor N. H. G. Robinson maintains, and most evangelicals would agree, that the idea of love as it is set forth in some current ethical discussions is inadequate to express the role of the Christian discipleship. "The demand of the present situation," he says, "is always much fuller than 'the principle of love' might lead us to expect. It is certainly true that the Christian life is a life of love, but it is equally the case that this is not the whole truth of the matter."[19] It is humanly impossible for a Christian or anyone else to maintain love as a constant expression of his personality. Does one "love" the driver who has just smashed into him? But when love fails, there remain duty and obedience to God. These, too, should be determinant factors in "situation ethics."

Principles of duty and obedience are not popular among today's new theologians; they prefer to speak of God entering the context of human behavior in "gull-like swoops,"[20] by which they seem to mean direct divine guidance in a particular situation. The abdication of moral principles is something no evangelical Christian can accept; and yet there is no question that examples of "situation ethics" can be found in the Bible. Jesus' question about lifting a sheep out of a pit on the sabbath day, and his citing of David's feeding of the troops at Nob with showbread, admit of such interpretation. The problems involved demand thoroughgoing study. There is enough truth in the idea of "situation ethics" to make it impressive, but not enough to justify the lengths to which it has been carried.

Similarly the concept of the "social ethic" is one that has acquired enormous prestige in our day, and it too carries Biblical truth that cannot be gainsaid. Jesus and the prophets before him took a special interest in the unfortunate, the friendless, and the helpless. The whole Bible could be considered from the sociological viewpoint a defense of the poor. Yet the personal ethic is as essential as the social ethic. The purity of a man's heart before God is never considered unimportant in Scripture. Homosexuality is hardly rated in the Bible on a moral level with "left-handedness," as was ventured by a British clergyman recently. The slavering and perverted sexuality on many newsstands would not be dismissed as "girlie books," as was done by an American clergyman who felt civil rights to be a far more important issue. Adultery and premarital sexual relations are not lightly regarded in Scripture; nor is immodesty of appearance. Without the New Testament personal ethic, the "social ethic" as currently espoused is in serious danger of gaining the whole world and losing its soul.

On the other hand, the evangelicals have a good deal to learn from the recent ethical theorists. Not all modern trends are unhealthy. There is no doubt that the Puritans were too "puritanical" and the Victorians too hypocritical, particularly in matters affecting sex. Christians cannot afford to be put into the Pharisaical position of condemning others' behavior. "For many years," writes Marshall McLuhan, "I have observed that the moralist typically substitutes anger for perception. He hopes that many people will mistake his irritation for insight."[21] The New Testament teaches that believers are to be moral but not moralistic. Instead of shaking the finger, instead of playing Mrs. Grundy with unbelievers, they are to win them to Christ. As Nicolas Berdyaev says, there are two kinds of moral enthusiasm. The first begins by demanding a high moral standard of oneself, the other by denouncing one's neighbor.[22]

Surely the new theologians are right in saying that the basis of Christian morality is neither pulchritude nor propriety nor the superego; it is love. They are right in asserting that sex in itself is a genuine good and that young people need to understand its potential. But they are wrong in their demeaning of virtue and their low view of the historic sanctions of the social order. Jesus Christ accepted moral standards. He upheld them as part of the fabric of God's love. He expected a high level of individual ethical conduct on the part of his disciples. Yet he was no inquisitor. The question the evangelical faces is: How can he discover an ethic that is truly the will of God for his own life, in his own time? And how can he make it an effective part of his personal and social witness for his Lord?

Chapter 11

The Defilement of the Earth

Dreaming alone of a people, dreaming alone of a day,
When men shall not rape my riches, and curse me and go away;
Making a bawd of my bounty, fouling the hand that gave—
Till I rise in my wrath and I sweep on their path and I stamp
    them into a grave.

Dreaming of men who will bless me, of women esteeming me good,
Of children born in my borders of radiant motherhood,
Of cities leaping to stature, of fame like a flag unfurled,
As I pour the tide of my riches in the eager lap of the world.

—Robert W. Service, "The Law of the Yukon"

Fifty-six swans rescued from the oil-polluted River Trent at
Burton, Staffordshire, were yesterday destroyed by workers of
the Royal Society for the Prevention of Cruelty to Animals.
Many were blinded by the oil. About 150 others will be cleaned
and freed later.

—*London Daily Express*, July 6, 1966

In the suburb of a midwestern city, newspapers reported, a housewife filled a glass of water from the tap at her sink and stared at it while a head of foam appeared. She repeated the act; the same thing occurred. City authorities were notified, other homes contacted, and an investigation was duly begun. The well from which the water was drawn, it was learned, had become contaminated by the increasing number of septic tanks in the area. Cleansing agents from neighborhood sewage had seeped through the soil into the drinking water supply.

In his Australian novel *On the Beach* Nevil Shute describes prophetically the final hours of the human race resulting from the outbreak of "World War III." The deadly dust from a thermonuclear exchange among the great powers drifts slowly southward, knocking out one Australian city after another. Finally a young scientist and his wife sit in their home in Melbourne, holding in their hands the capsules that will when swallowed deliver them from the approaching horror.

"Couldn't anyone have stopped it?" asks the wife. She looks pitifully at the child to whom they have just given a fatal injection.

"We were all too silly," says her husband.[1]

The Bible has a good deal to say about Heaven, but it has even more to say about the earth. The attitude of the sacred writers toward the earth was strangely affectionate. It is obvious that they loved it and appreciated its bounty. The very first book describes the Creator looking upon this planet with its fertile grass, its herbs and trees, and seeing that it was good. In the final book the angels are warned by the Great Judge not to hurt the earth, the grass, the trees, or the sea. The psalmist composes some of his most beautiful lyrics about the earth as a place overflowing with riches and goodness and love and praise. The earth is honored by the presence of Deity: "He visits the earth and waters it."[2] The earth is filled with divine glory and blessed with life-giving powers. From the dust of the earth man was first formed. He was put on the earth to till and replenish it, and to sustain himself from its bountiful supply. The most beloved of all the psalms is a picture of domesticated animals, green pastures, and still waters—the earth.

But the Bible also contains a stern warning: "Defile not the land which ye shall inhabit, wherein I dwell: for I the Lord dwell among the children of Israel."[3] Defilement means to render unholy that which is holy, or make impure that which is pure. The concept is applied Scripturally to men, to women, to the house of worship, to the sabbath, and to the dwelling place. It is also applied to the earth; and Isaiah mourns that "the earth also is defiled under the inhabitants . . . because they have transgressed the laws."[4] What are the marks of defilement? Joel speaks of wasted fields and wasted grain; Isaiah of wasted rivers and wasted cities. The Bible paints many pictures of the earth come under judgment as a result of man's sin. The most terrible, perhaps, is contained in Deuteronomy 28. Studying it in the 1960's, one gets the eerie feeling that the ancient Hebrews must have been given a good peek behind the curtain of time:

If you will not obey the voice of the Lord your God or be careful to do all his commandments . . . cursed shall you be in the city, and cursed shall you be in the field. Cursed shall be your basket and your kneading-trough. Cursed shall be the fruit of your body, and the fruit of your ground, the increase of your cattle, and the young of your flock. Cursed shall you be when you come in, and cursed shall you be when you go out.

The Lord will send upon you curses, confusion, and frustration, in all that you undertake to do, until you are destroyed and perish quickly, on account of the evil of your doings. . . . The Lord will make the pestilence cleave to you until he has consumed you off the land. . . . The Lord will smite you with consumption, and with fever, inflammation, and fiery heat, and with drought, and with blasting, and with mildew. . . . And the heavens over your head shall be brass, and the earth under you shall be iron. The Lord will make the rain of your land powder and dust; from heaven it shall come down upon you until you are destroyed.[5]

A modern writer, Alan Paton, has reflected the stern words of the Pentateuch in his story of South Africa: "The ground is holy, being even as it came from the Creator. Keep it, guard it, care for it, for it keeps men, guards men, cares for men. Destroy it and man is destroyed."[6]

Jesus of Nazareth loved the earth. The Gospels record that he knelt upon it and slept on it. He ate and drank from it. He walked through it, admired its beauty, and told stories about it. Jesus did not countenance wastefulness. He rebuked, in effect, the prodigal son who wasted his substance, and the steward who wasted his master's goods.[7] "Every one to whom much is given, of him will much be required."[8] Jesus spoke often of the promises of God to be fulfilled in the next life for those who believed in him; but he also spoke of the divine Protector who gave the wild creatures their food and shelter in this life. He reminded men in parable after parable of their obligation to take care of what was entrusted to them. Those who were faithful in husbanding their responsibilities, he said, would be acceptable for nobler duties.

There is nothing complicated about either the Old or New Testament teaching regarding the care of the earth; it makes as much sense outside the church as inside. The Bible is not of course a book of conservation but of salvation. Yet the two are not alien to each other. The foam in the water glass and the appalling prediction in Nevil Shute's novel reveal the present direction that human folly is taking, in complete contravention of the whole thrust of the Bible. Man, as the United States Senator from Wisconsin observes, has an infinite capacity for fouling his environment.[9] The Scripture speaks of man not as good, nor yet as essentially bad, but rather as a good thing spoiled; and there is danger that the same may soon be said of the earth he inhabits. Expanding industry is turning rivers into waste canals and lakes into quagmires; creatures of the land are perishing by the millions under the relentless advance of the population; the ocean is being stripped of its noblest species by commercial interests; prairies are being denuded of life by unwise land use; even song birds are being driven from the woods and butterflies from the meadows; while the air above us is turning noxious from the fumes of thousands of factories and a billion combustion engines. All without benefit of mushroom clouds or atomic fallout!

In many places on this planet the majesty of God's created order is still visible. The fugitive from traffic can, if he ventures far enough, still catch his breath at the wonder of forest and shoreline. The Joshua tree still blossoms on the desert, the heather on the hills. The Douglas fir still drops its needles on the mountain saddle. Wherever his treasure is not yet plundered, God drapes his earth in splendor and quiet beauty. Even where ancient man laid waste the land, time has discreetly covered the debris with a rug of dust. Cities come and cities go, but Mother Earth has remained on the whole friendly and hospitable to life. If men have made "a bawd of her bounty," she has not minded too much.

But that is the world that was, the world that is disappearing, the world before automation. And what do we have left? "Cans. Beer cans. Glinting on the verges of a million miles of roadways, lying in scrub, grass, dirt, leaves, sand, mud, but never hidden. Piels, Rheingold, Ballantine, Schaefer, Schlitz, shining in the sun or picked by moon or the beams of headlights at night; washed by rain or flattened by wheels, but never dulled, never buried, never destroyed." Here, as Marya Mannes says, is "the mark of the savages, the testament of wasters, the stain of posterity."[10]

The Christian who builds his life on the Bible looks for the Lord Jesus Christ to come in power one day and to establish a new heaven and a new earth. Meanwhile—and the whole problem of the evangelical's social conscience is bound up in that word "meanwhile." For whether he likes it or not, he is bound in stewardship to take care of this earth until he gets a better one. To sit in a church pew and contemplate the glory to come is one of the quiet joys of the believer's life; but even here the desecration of the earth intrudes. Smog makes the worshiper's eyes smart, so that he cannot read his Bible; and even as he watches the candidates for membership present themselves, he realizes that they are being baptized in water that is the next thing to contaminated. There is no escape! Fifty years ago Christians often spoke of spiritual withdrawal from the world, but today scientists are telling us that it is the earth itself that is withdrawing. Says S. P. R. Charter, "The land gradually withdraws from the abuse it has received at the hand of man who does not plan or accept responsibility for his own future."[11]

The Gospel remains the hope of earth and the joy of heaven, and the only answer to the problems of life; but the question of the disciple's involvement is no longer debatable. We are all involved, whether we like it or not. A few facts will illustrate:

Water. Because it is the most widely used resource in the world, the demand for water increases approximately twice as rapidly as does population. In the United States today approximately three-fourths of the human population lives with a chronic water shortage, poor water quality, or a combination of both. The city of Chicago is continually asking for more water from Lake Michigan because of rising industrial needs. The lake has reached a dangerously low level; health hazards and the future of marine life are involved. An annual influx of 400,000 persons into the state of California has multiplied its water requirements, particularly in the more arid south. The counties of northern California are demanding replenishment of the state water supply from the Pacific Northwest watersheds before releasing additional water to the huge population to the south. In the Rockies, the state of Colorado is insisting upon replenishment of its water supply from the Columbia River basin before permitting the state of Arizona to drain additional waters from the Colorado River. The great metropolitan areas of the eastern seaboard, notably New York City, Philadelphia, and Washington, D. C., are suffering for lack of adequate water reserves.

The current rate of withdrawal of water from underground reservoirs throughout America is many times the rate of its replenishment. Water tables are dropping in Texas, Arizona, California, and elsewhere; saline water is creeping in from the sea, and even the best-designed pumps are yielding in some areas only a flow of unusable water. The use of nuclear energy to obtain clear water from the ocean cheaply is apparently no final solution. Scientists say that the problems of nuclear fission may mount; radioactive material may find its way into the waterways, and man and beast will then be worse off than before. Quite apart from the threat of future radioactivity, Senator Gaylord Nelson of Wisconsin, quoted earlier, has estimated that it will cost the United States from $50 to $100 billion just to clean up its turgid rivers and lakes so that they will be fit once again for use by living creatures.[12]

In many parts of the world grim struggles are shaping up over the use of river water, reminiscent of the old cattle feuds in the western plains of the United States, which often concerned water rights. The prophet Isaiah describes the peace of God as being "like a river," but the truth of unregenerate human nature is that men will fight for water. It is not without significance that Jesus blessed the man who shared the water that was his.

Land. In 1798 Thomas Robert Malthus, a 28-year-old English economist, published a lengthy pamphlet entitled, *An Essay on the Principle of Population as It Affects the*

Future Improvement of Society. In this booklet young Malthus put forward the view that population, when unchecked, increases in geometrical ratio, whereas subsistence increases only in arithmetical ratio. It was a pessimistic booklet and aroused great controversy at the time. Today the specter of overpopulation is stalking the planet in earnest, and the sinister Malthusian principle has taken on new significance. By the year 2000 A.D. the world population will total over six billion persons according to present predictions. In the past the earth has been a good pantry, but tomorrow there just will not be enough land available for cultivation to provide food for the demographic explosion. Much of the soil has been subject to mistreatment. Indiscriminate land use has caused and still causes the erosion of topsoil and the loss of hundreds of thousands of acres of arable land. Placer dredges and strip mining have gouged up some of the finest river bottom land and created a landscape over vast areas as desolate as a moon crater. And of course dust storms, smog, floods, and drought have severely affected recent harvests in many parts of the world.

In spite of the Bible teaching that the earth is the Lord's, evangelical Christians have had very little to say about man's care of the land. Men strip a forest or burn it, and they move on; they work a claim until it peters out or until the earth has caved in, and they move on; they exhaust the soil through carelessness and greed, and they move on. In the past, if some conservationist raised his voice in protest against such behavior, he was called an enemy of progress. In fact, warnings about the misuse of natural resources have often resulted in actual acceleration of the stripping pace, such is the perversity of human nature. But times change, and there is not much sand left in the sandpile for the children to play with. Christians who think of themselves as stewards of the mysteries of Grace are, by the same dispensation, stewards of the realities of earth. Their search for a "better country" in Heaven does not justify their littering or spoiling this one while they are here—or allowing others to do so if it is possible to stop it.

Malthus maintained that the real problem was not the land or the food supply; the real problem was people—ever-increasing numbers of them. Books on the subject of population control are now rolling off the presses nearly every week, underscoring the seriousness of the crisis. The time is long past due for evangelical Christians to be taking a public stand on the issue of birth control. To add to the spate of volumes is not necessary; what is needed is some indication that there is a Bible-centered point of view in the matter, based on the desire of God for the welfare of man, and on principles of Christian stewardship. At the turn of the century, when evangelicals thought of birth control at all, they condemned it as contrary to nature. Such a position is no longer tenable; the place is simply getting too crowded.

Air. The Australian picture painted by Nevil Shute in *On the Beach* is so similar to the dread prophecy in Deuteronomy and to the record of what happened to Sodom and Gomorrah that evangelical Christians who look for the end times should be keenly aware of the current crisis in air pollution. Millions of dollars have been spent in studies of the problem in Europe and America, and some strides have been taken to lessen air contamination. Yet the ever-multiplying demands of industry are so fouling the air above our population centers that the health of the citizenry is now seriously at stake. It is a social issue of the first magnitude, and many Christian laymen are engaged in the effort to clear the air through scientific controls; yet somehow the evangelical churches have not considered it their problem. They have not faced the fact that the preaching of the Gospel itself is threatened when the air is unfit for breathing.

The ordinary pollutants created by technology are beginning to make life miserable in our cities. But what of the cloud of nuclear dust that has been circling the earth ever since the first atmospheric explosion at Los Alamos, and steadily drifting down in radioactive rain and dust to contaminate everything on the earth's surface, including those whom the Lord has anointed? More nations rush to join the thermonuclear club, more explosions are set off, and more deadly radiation enters the atmosphere. Is the believer a sheep, or a head of lettuce, that he should submit to this spoliation of nature without uttering a warning in the name of the Lord? Is there no social conscience in him to care what happens to the whole human race for whom Christ died? Simon de Montfort put every inhabitant of a city in southern France to the sword, whether heretic or orthodox, because he said, "The Lord knows his own." Lenin was willing to sacrifice half the world's population to advance his particular theories of socialism. In the face of today's mounting threat of total erasure, what does the evangelical Christian propose? A well-supplied, air-conditioned cave?

There are ways of dealing with the vexing problems of water shortage and pollution, and many governments and industries are hard at work on proposed solutions. United programs exist which can be put into operation to contain the explosive birth rate, to preserve natural resources, and to reclaim land for greater food production. These are being implemented. International agreements are even being sought to reduce the danger of air contamination, atomic and otherwise. Tremendous energy is going into the efforts to find viable answers. The challenge to the evangelical is not to seek some esoteric panacea of his own, but to put his shoulder to the wheel and get into the struggle as a working member of twentieth-century society. He has a contribution to make; in the name of the Lord, let him make it!

Some day this earthly environment will pass away. God

has left us no timetable as to when life on this planet will cease and the scroll be rolled up. Christians believe that the hour may be soon coming when they will go forth to meet the Lord at his second advent. The Apostle Paul says that the whole creation "waits with eager longing" for that day when it will be "set free from its bondage to decay."[13] Until that consummation takes place the faithful disciple has an obligation to the created order. As one in whom the image of God has been restored by Grace, he is to share in the divine mercy. He is to teach his fellows that "if man is to feed all the hungry and help the desert to blossom as the rose and, indeed, if he is to survive, he has to be not just scientific, he has to be reverent."[14] As Edward Hyams says, man cannot really control nature. "He can gain his commodity by cooperating with her and in no other way."[15] To upset the rhythm and balance of nature is not our option. Luther told his students that if he knew for certain that the world would end tomorrow, his duty today would require him to plant his garden—and to collect the rent!

God put his children here to take care of what is his and theirs—namely, the earth—until he takes them out of it for something better. There is no escaping responsibility. Christians are to work, to plant, to build, to pray, and to bring men to God while it is day, for the night cometh when no man can work.

Chapter 12

Blessed Are the Peacemakers

Paz en la tierra a los hombres de buena voluntad.
(Peace on earth among men of good will.)

—Luke 2:14

*Inscription on a cross placed on the summit of Mt. Whitney,
California by a team of Mexican climbers, July 1967.*

The evangelical Christian wants peace. He has been branded
a warmonger, a misanthrope, a sadist, and a cynic, sometimes with malice, sometimes with truth; but in his proper
role he is none of them. Were an honorable cease-fire to be
arranged today in the Republic of Vietnam that would give
the people of that country a chance for a free and productive
life, he would be the first to his knees in thanksgiving. He
would like nothing better than a world in which he could
bring up his children with no fear other than the fear and
admonition of the Lord. Any slightest slackening of the arms
race; any reduction of international tensions; any agreement
that would end the tragic casualty lists and halt radioactive
fallout, he would warmly welcome—

Provided!

And that word "provided" makes all the difference. It
sets him apart from many of the people who are taking part
in the great peace debate today. The evangelical is not nor-

113

mally disillusioned by human nature to the extent of becoming a pessimist. But there is, or should be, a quality of hard realism that marks his attitude in the current discussions of peace. It is based primarily on memory. The evangelical keeps remembering history.

In July 1929 President Herbert Hoover promulgated the Kellogg-Briand Peace Pact, which formally renounced the use of war as an instrument of national policy for the settling of disputes between nations. Forty-five sovereign states signed that document at the time. Their leaders made spectacular references to "peace on earth" in speeches before their respective national assemblies. Two years later Japan, one of the signatories, sent an armed invasion into Manchuria. Another two years passed, and Hitler swept into power in Germany, introducing the *blitzkrieg* as an instrument of national policy. World War II was the result. In September 1938 Prime Minister Neville Chamberlain returned from Munich to greet the London crowds with the assurance of "peace in our time." He had just signed a four-party agreement giving Germany the right to invade and occupy portions of Czechoslovakia. For the sake of maintaining peace in Europe, the Prime Minister had gone against his better judgment. He felt justified in sacrificing principle to avoid another blood-bath. He wanted earnestly to do the right thing. World War II was the result.

The evangelical is certainly not the only one who remembers the sobering events of the recent past. He has no claim to special wisdom in interpreting those events. His contribution, if it can be called that, consists of what he has found in the Old and New Testaments. In the thirteenth chapter of Mark Jesus is quoted as predicting that the future would contain "wars and rumors of wars," with "nation rising against nation, and kingdom against kingdom."[1] The Apostle James asks in his epistle, "What causes wars, and what causes fightings among you? Is it not your passions that are at war in your members? You desire and do not have; so you kill. And you covet and cannot obtain; so you fight and wage war."[2] The statesmen of the various nations put their signatures to the Kellogg-Briand agreement in 1929 without concentrating (as Madison did in 1789) on the problem of the sin of man. They neglected to take into account the unregenerate heart that lusts for power over other people. They did not even calculate their own *hubris*, the self-interest and nationalistic pride that is so willing to trample on the rights of others to gain its own ends. They just signed and hoped for the best.

But Jesus knew what was in man. He taught his followers that there are demons of pride and lust that must be driven out of people's hearts before there can be a willingness to make peace. He knew also how powerless men are against such evil. So he went to the cross—the just for the unjust—to do what had to be done, and there made a full, perfect, and sufficient sacrifice for the sins of men. How beautiful upon the mountains then are the feet of him that bringeth good tidings, that publisheth peace, that bringeth good tidings of good![3] How glorious that, even in a day of mounting international confusion, because of what Christ has done the peace of God can flow into the soul of man. Today all over the world—including those areas where all the horrors of war are present—people are finding victory through the Lord Jesus Christ. Reconciliation is being effected through faithful servants of his Gospel. The demons are being exorcised; sin is being forgiven; hatred is being expelled by love. Without this peace in the heart, there can never be peace among the nations. Jesus himself set the order of priority: "Have salt in yourselves, and be at peace one with another."[4] That inner peace,

established by the Grace of God, is the only true peace
that this planet will know until the Prince of Peace comes
at the Second Advent to set up his reign. So the Bible
teaches; so the evangelical believes.

There is, however, another word on the subject. Our
Lord has left his followers a mandate they cannot evade:
"Blessed are the peacemakers, for they shall be called sons
of God."[5] No artificial withdrawal from the world is evident here; no contracting out of the social issues that
divide men. Jesus is calling his disciples to accept responsibility for the resolving of political, economic, and social
conflicts in the working out of peace. In so doing he is not
overthrowing the concept of holiness. There is perhaps
some misunderstanding as to what the Bible means by
"separation from the world." The purpose of separation is
not to make the believer into an ascetic superman or some
kind of solo spook. Separation equips the Christian with
the weapons of his warfare. It gives him the armor and
the matériel to wage his campaign against evil. Instead of
getting him out of the world, it gets him into the world
more effectively and keeps him from being sidetracked.
The sharper the separation, the more impenetrable the
armor, the greater the dependence upon Christ and the
more fruitful the involvement.

Words like "armor" and "warfare" are not taken from
the vocabulary of peace, but the Bible uses them with
good reason. It looks at life more as a battleground than
a peace conference. It speaks of spiritual wickedness in
high places, and of a cosmic struggle against the principal-
ities and powers of darkness. But it also says that the battle
and the victory are the Lord's. "I am the Lord; I make
peace."[6]

The first condition that the evangelical would postulate,
then, as he joins the quest for peace is, "provided it be

understood that man as presently constituted is incapable of achieving peace."[7] A military armistice or a political treaty may stop men from killing each other for a few days or months or years, but the Bible teaches that it will not bring peace. Elaborate proposals for utopias such as the "classless society" of Marxism will not bring peace. Marxism suffers from the same ideological taint it has detected in other social systems. Were the nations of the world to agree on January 1, 1984 to dismantle their bombers and fighter planes, convert their tanks into tractors, take their armies out of uniform, and send their conventional and thermonuclear hardware to Venus in a one-way rocket, they would all begin rearming—probably before nightfall. Such rearming would be undertaken surreptitiously, in violation of the most solemn obligations; but it would be done. The Kellogg-Briand Pact posited a goodness in man that the Word of God and the facts of human nature will not support. Each new generation displays its own forms of the traditional bias in man toward weakness, pride, greed, and lust. Nothing can prevent it, nothing except—

The evangelical attaches a second important condition to his desire for peace. He wants such peace as men can attain to have some kind of relationship to justice. He observes many different kinds of peace prevailing in the world he inhabits. Not all of them are good. For example, there is the peace that death brings, the peace of the tomb. Today it could be called the peace of Auschwitz. Hitler tried to "make peace" with the Jews by seeking their "final solution"; but the evangelical would rather fight than submit to such a peace. There is also the peace of slavery and subjection, the Pax Romana. Dictators are very fond of the Roman peace. Today it could be called the peace of Tibet. The nation of Tibet has been completely stripped of its personality in our generation by Communist China without a single protest being made in front of a single embassy. There is peace in Tibet, but the Tibetans would end it if they could. Again, there is peace that is artificially induced in men. Among individuals it is the peace of the tranquilizer, the peace of withdrawal and schizophrenia, the peace of the brainwashed prisoner. Should large-scale chemical warfare break out, we are told, whole cities could be sprayed and pacified by such drugs. The evangelical is not interested in paying such high prices for the sake of peace. He would rather stay free, and alive, and in his right mind, prepared to fight. "There are many things worse than war," Winston Churchill once said. "Slavery is worse than war. Dishonor is worse than war." He was echoing the words of John Stuart Mill: "War is an ugly thing, but not the ugliest of things: the decayed and degraded state of moral and patriotic feeling which thinks nothing *worth* a war is worse. . . . A man who has nothing which he cares more about than he does about his personal safety is a miserable creature who has no chance of being free, unless made and kept so by the exertions of better men than himself."[8]

If there is to be peace, the evangelical feels it cannot be at the expense of a victimized people. Such a vindictive peace only contains the seeds of future wars. History affords many examples of the enlightened peace; it is not something impossible of attainment. Alfred's attitude toward the Danes in the year 878, Lincoln's sympathy for the South during the closing days of the Civil War, and MacArthur's treatment of the Japanese in 1945 show what can be done when the desire to heal wounds is greater than the desire to exact retribution after the firing has ceased.

Because of their strong theological expressions, and because they are not always as tactful and gracious as they should be, the evangelicals' position is sometimes cast in an unfavorable light. In 1965 the *Christian Century* magazine wanted to know, "Are there any neoevangelicals who are not in full support of [the United States] government's policy in South Vietnam (or of any other national-militarist program of our government)?"[9] The editorial equated the "neo-evangelical" with simple nationalism, and his peace aims with the foreign policy of the current administration. Such criticism is probably healthy because it forces Christian thinking, but it is inadequate because it fails to spell out the alternatives open to peace-seeking people. To clear the air, some of the free world's options are here briefly set forth.

1. *Neutrality.* The policy of neutrality is one that has been adopted by a number of nations who have powerful neighbors. Some neutrals are heavily armed, some are not. Normally neutrality is not considered a viable stance for an individual living under the obligations of citizenship.

2. *Pacifism.* From earliest times there have been pacifist elements in the church, and today some of the strongest evangelical churches are committed to the pacifist position. Certain branches of the Brethren, Mennonites and Quakers are examples. Numerous governments (none of them Communist) recognize the right of citizens to refuse combatant service on religious grounds. With their churches' approval, some conscientious objectors enlist in noncombatant military activities, while others accept assignments to supervised work of national importance. Evangelicals have come to honor the convictions of the religiously motivated pacifists even when disagreeing with their interpretation of Scripture.

3. *Marxism.* As one who holds a doctrinaire commitment to the concept of class warfare, the true Marxist does not believe in peace. To him peace is supremely a weapon in the ideological war. The present party line makes it expedient for Marxists living on both sides of the Iron Curtain to adopt the posture of peaceableness toward certain

major powers. They hope thereby to lull their enemies into relaxing their guard. The internal history of the world Communist movement is evidence that such peace as it achieves is gained only at the expense of humanity. As the Marxist bends with dignity to lay a wreath on the monument to peace, many people (but not evangelicals) are shocked to find that there is gore on his hands. The hands are quickly covered, and people soon forget about it.

4. *Indifferentism.* Following the thought of Bertrand Russell and others, many men today are convinced that survival itself is a desirable goal. They hold that existence is the supreme good; that peace should be sought therefore at any price. Political freedom is demeaned. It is felt that in time man can always throw off whatever yoke of servitude is thrust upon him as a result of his indifference toward tyranny. Some describe the position as "better Red than dead." It can be used, and has been used, to set the stage for a Communist usurpation of power.

5. *Appeasement.* This position represents a backing down in the face of hostile military power, based upon considerations of fear or prudence. Those who favor appeasement do not consider the experience of Munich in 1938 to be applicable to Southeast Asia today. They favor territorial concessions to the Communists. They recommend unilateral nuclear disarmament by the United States. They hold that world Communism is fragmenting; that soon the Communist countries will be enjoying moderate freedom. The new missile installations in Cuba are not regarded as dangerous. They consider Communists to be peace-loving people and doubt that Communism needs to be "contained"; and in any event they consider such containment impossible in Asia.

6. *Strategic retreat.* In the Vietnam issue, which has divided the free world, many who cannot by any stretch of

imagination be called "appeasers" have come to the con-
clusion that American and allied assistance has proved a
tragic mistake. Spearheaded by church groups and members
of the academic community in the United States, and backed
by mass media and public opinion in many other countries,
this point of view is dedicated to the removal of American
and allied troops from Southeast Asia. The action, it is
tacitly recognized, would probably result in a Communist
take-over. Such a development however is considered less
dangerous to world peace than the continued "illegal" and
"immoral" build-up of American forces in Asia.

Sponsors of the view are not necessarily pacifistic; many
of them endorsed the Israeli invasion of the Arab countries
in June 1967. They oppose the war in Southeast Asia because they see it as a large nation (the U.S.A.) turning its big
guns on a small nation (North Vietnam) in a part of the
world where they believe the large nation has no business
to be. Sickened by television's revelation of the killing and
maiming that accompanies modern war, they appeal to
humanitarian instincts, claiming that the American military leaders are drawing the whole world into a blood-
bath. They believe that retreat is the only way to avoid it.
They see no need for a countervailing force in Southeast
Asia to press for peaceful political change in place of the
usual Communist pattern of violent "liberation." However,
many who favor American withdrawal from Vietnam take
a moderate view as to how it should be done. They profess
no desire to see the people of the Republic of Vietnam
abandoned completely to the mercies of Hanoi and the National Liberation Front. They would insist, they say, upon
some form of continuing protection being provided. On the
other hand they tend to ignore the statements of Red China's
and Cuba's leaders that the latter intend to start more "Viet-
nams" around the world, particularly in Asia, Africa, and

Latin America, for the purpose of "bleeding America to death."

7. *Over-the-brinkmanship.* This term serves as well as any to describe a position that calls for all-out aggressive action. It goes beyond "eyeball-to-eyeball" diplomacy to prescribe swift military invasion and air attacks on neutral targets. It places undue reliance on military force to bring about the reduction of international tensions. Under certain conditions it could recommend the use of tactical nuclear weapons for offensive purposes. It leans to the belief that the one hope for peace is to take the enemy by surprise and destroy him.

8. *Revolution.* A young generation reared in affluence is beginning to move in many directions. One is the elimination of the dislocations of society by direct acts of pressure and violence. While a few radical churchmen are associated with these "new left" groups, most of their leaders are skeptical in attitude if not atheistic. A study of the doctrine of man as they hold it would probably reveal that they have picked up their pointers on human nature from a museum of anthropology. God, they would say, is dead. Such groups may not always be led directly by Communist cadres, but their prejudices and aims are similar. To burn flags, destroy draft cards, stone embassies, halt troop trains, incite riots, invade schools, and defy the law is a part of their revolution against the "establishment" and the "power structures." They would asserts that their object is to bring about justice and peace.

The evangelical considers these eight options with their various combinations and overlappings, hoping that some of them will offer a better solution to the present dilemma than the option to which he is now committed: support of the Republic of Vietnam in its struggle for independence and democratic government, and resistance to Communist aggression in Southeast Asia. He finds that the New Testament has a bias toward the "doves" rather than the "hawks," but that in the last analysis God alone remains Lord of the Christian conscience. As a redeemed Christian he feels a great debt of gratitude to the free land that nurtured him, trained his mind and his body, put up with his youthful foibles, and gave him the blessings of a goodly heritage. He wants to protect his nation's good against those who seem so eager to take it away for something "better."

What does the evangelical think about the options listed? He knows he cannot be neutral in a divided world. For the most part he cannot adopt the pacifist position, much as he may admire it, because he considers it an unwarranted retreat from the power struggle.[10] On the other hand he finds the Bible opposed to aggressive militarism. The concept of the holy war is foreign to the New Testament and to much of the Old Testament. "Not by might nor by power but by my Spirit, saith the Lord."[11] Thus he concludes that extreme "hawkishness" or "over-the-brinkmanship" in the late twentieth century has run out of spiritual fuel as well as common sense.

Marxism the evangelical rejects because of its utopianism and because at its heart it is at mortal enmity with God. Appeasement he believes would be a prelude to Communist world power moves that would precipitate a reign of terror. The clamor for Allied withdrawal from Vietnam, whether or not it is Communist-inspired, represents to him an unrealistic appraisal of the total world situation and an unwillingness to face the radical nature of evil. Indifference he thinks of as simply another form of surrender. Because he is deeply committed to the cause of Christian morality, he finds it difficult to understand why the act of a large nation in coming to the aid of a beleaguered, friendly small nation is considered immoral. He is puzzled because so many of those who are pointing up the moral issue in Vietnam made no protest when the Baltic states were swallowed up by Russia, when Berlin was blockaded, when Tibet was raped, when the Republic of Korea was attacked, when Hungary was overrun, when Cuba was invaded, when Goa was seized by India, or when Britain drove the Communists out of Malaysia. Were these not immoral acts by the same standard? Yet they met with scant opposition.

The evangelical believes that the fashion of this world is passing away.

> The tumult and the shouting dies,
> The captains and the kings depart.[12]

He looks upon this world as a proving ground for a better one. He involves himself in the sociopolitical order, shorn of perfectionist illusions, but hoping to achieve some positive goals and a measure of peace for mankind. He links the struggle for social justice to man's emancipation from his own nature. He finds no evidence in Scripture that man can be transformed by altering his environment. Here he nails down the great fallacy of Marxism; for the dialectical materialists have never understood the truth about human nature. They have defined man as producing animal but have not identified man as sinner. As Berdyaev says, "The sinfulness of human nature does not mean that social reforms and improvements are impossible. It only means that there can be no perfect and absolute social order . . . before the transfiguration of the world."[13]

The evangelical in the Western world believes deeply in freedom. He follows Calvin rather than Luther in holding that political freedom derives from the spiritual freedom imparted by Christ. He considers that the only progress man ever makes is progress toward God. It is true that some orthodox Christians, ever since the days of Origen, have been speculating that "if everyone were saved, wars would stop, crime and poverty would disappear, and life would become heaven on earth." That opinion is not held by the majority

of evangelicals. They pin their hopes not on wishful thinking but on the possibilities that God can bring about in the
context of human freedom. That is why they strive to keep
the borders open, to avoid open clashes. To be effective,
evangelism must be heard, and how can it be heard in an
atmosphere of violence? Passionate men, hot-blooded bat-
tlers, men in a killing mood, are not very susceptible to the
sound of the Gospel. Anger will not make an entrance for
God's Word. So the Christian seeks peace that the Gospel
may have free course.

The Vietnam question really belongs in the framework of
human freedom. Seen thus, it does not become a matter of
fighting in Saigon to avoid fighting in Seattle. Nor can it be
written off purely as a boon to the stock market, or a struggle
to maintain the balance of power, or an orgy of mass stupidity,
or the useless sacrifice of the flower of youth. It cannot even be
described completely as big neighbor helping little neighbor.
Vietnam becomes rather the same basic issue that free men
have faced in two World Wars and Korea: *Will a man fight
for his freedom? Because if he won't, in a sinful planet he
will not have it long.*

For the Christian believer the decision to support any war
is agonizing; who can claim to follow the Lord of Glory
and rejoice in the wanton wasting of human life, the most
precious thing in creation? It is in such a context that the
evangelical regards the United Nations. A drowning man will
clutch at a straw, even though he knows it is a straw and
that it will not save him. The United Nations is a weak
instrument unable to deliver according to the terms of its
charter; yet now is not the time to abandon it. The threads
of hope may be fragile, but the evangelical is called to
strengthen them. Some consider that because the United
Nations Organization officially ignores the deity, it is a
worldly and satanic vehicle with which Christians should

have nothing to do. Perhaps if they were sitting in the White House, burdened with the responsibility for the welfare and safety of two hundred million persons of all races and religious views, and obligated at the same time to allied nations and to the whole world, they would temper their views.

When he has made his decision to take part in war, the Christian will find that the soldier's profession is an honorable one.[14] Many men have served God and country well in arms; they have been valorous in battle, magnanimous in victory, patient in defeat and capture, and faithful in death. As horrible as war is, there are nevertheless conventions which some civilized warring nations (assuming the two adjectives are not mutually exclusive) have agreed to observe. The soldier, as such nations conceive of him, is not called upon to exercise cruelty in carrying out his duties. The Christian would go farther to say that mistreatment of enemy wounded or prisoners of war, individual acts of brutality and terrorism, or indifference toward the safety of civilian populations do not constitute proper military behavior under any conditions. There is nothing Christian, patriotic, honorable, or even human about the wartime actions of military or civilian personnel who choose to violate these conventions, or who use the cloak of war to cover their own sadistic impulses.

Further, there is nothing in the Bible that says that because a Christian is called to war, he has to develop a pugnacious disposition or a pugilistic outlook on life. Some of the greatest men of combat, as has been mentioned, have been even greater men of peace. In battle dress they have added new dignity to the term, "Christian gentlemen."

The eighth option of our list remains to be considered. A new generation is gathering at the gates of power, and some of its leaders are transfixed with the idea that peace and justice will come through a different kind of war, namely, social revolution. In Tokyo, in Jakarta, in Cochabamba, in Moscow and Havana, in Paris, Cambridge, Regina, Accra, in New York City—wherever students meet, there is talk of the revolutionary day in which men live. A buoyant optimism pervades these groups, much of it due to the exuberance of youth. They chant, "We're going to change the world"— and indeed they may. But when all the changes and upheavals of the twentieth century have taken place, will the world then be more just? Will there be peace? The evangelical wishes it were true, but his sources of wisdom indicate otherwise. The sad history of the world is that things will be different, but they will not necessarily be better, and they may be worse. Was Nkhrumah so much better than the British, or Sukarno than the Dutch? Is Castro so much better than Batista?

The Bible teaches that neither youth nor age, nor black nor white man nor church nor state, is going to build the peaceful new society that people have dreamed and struggled and marched for. That society is going to come full-bodied from the hand of God himself in his own time. What the twentieth century has to work with is a world that has come of age technologically, but is wavering emotionally between infancy and senile dementia. The opportunities for advance were never greater than now; yet some of the revolutionary leadership provided by the "social guerillas" is proving irresponsible and anarchic.

But not all! There are many young evangelicals who are also convinced that some kind of social revolution could help change the world for good and increase the possibilities of peace. They are dissatisfied with the ominous build-up on both sides in Vietnam. They agree that the bomb is only a surface lesion of a more serious disorder within the human heart, and that a ban-the-bomb parade can therefore never achieve its goal, though it were to march to the moon and back. They know that the world is warped by sin, and that only the Grace of God can free men from their grandiose illusions and their despair. They know that true peace will only come with the return of the Prince of Peace. But they ask, "Does that mean nothing can be done? What about the love we have for people? What about the Holy Spirit whose fruits are love, joy, peace, and goodness? Why did Jesus say, 'Blessed are the peacemakers'? Who is to keep us from putting on the shoes of the preparation of the Gospel of peace,[15] and going out to win men everywhere to Christ's banner of love?"

Chapter 13

Making a Stab at the Issues

The anguish of the world is on my tongue.
My bowl is filled to the brim with it; there is more than I can eat.

—Edna St. Vincent Millay

Social problems exist wherever men exist. The evangelical is not teacher's pet; he has no privileged corner in the universe. Our Lord pointed out that the rain falls on the just and unjust.[1] Nor does the evangelical have a vest-pocket solution to every towering issue that comes along. He does have Jesus; he believes that Jesus is adequate to meet human need at every level; and he believes that to know Christ is to have a head start in grappling with the dilemmas that society poses. He does not, however, confuse dilemma-grappling with the process of coming to know Christ; that is, he does not consider social action to be the same thing as evangelism. Evangelism is presenting Christ to men in the power of the Holy Spirit. Social action is an effort to apply Christ in finding solutions to human problems. When social action is mistaken for evangelism the church has ceased to manufacture its own blood cells and is dying of leukemia. When social action becomes more important than evangelism the church has forgotten to breathe and is already dead of heart failure.

Yet every human being has to face, every day of his life,

problems calling for some kind of social action. And no matter how rich his spiritual resources may be, a Christian can still become confused simply by a lack of information. What does one do when the Bible appears to be silent on a particular matter? If he turns to secular authorities the answer may be, and frequently is, shocking. If he picks up an ethical survey to determine right from wrong, it may be filled with relativities; or it may be too theoretical to be of practical use. Some justification exists, therefore, for discussing in the following pages, however sketchily, social matters that have gone unmentioned or have been briefly referred to thus far. The comments are not intended to be final. Rather it is hoped they will initiate a discussion within the evangelical community that will show that the Bible is indeed a living document for our day. It is also hoped that they will create an appetite for further literature on the subject.

CHURCH AND STATE

While evangelical Christians honor and respect high churchmen who honor the Lord Jesus Christ, and count them brethren,[2] the typical evangelical is apt to be a low churchman who views church control of the state and state control of the church with an equally baleful eye. Memories of persecution die slowly in his heart. He talks about the need for a wall of separation between church and state much as Thomas Jefferson talked about it. But the world refuses to stand still, and changes are taking place that now appear to be threatening some of the old distinctions. In Britain and the United States and other countries there is a swing toward the complete secularization of life. Theism— the simple belief in God—is under heavy fire. Protestant-Catholic hostility is thawing; many of the lines that once divided religious communities are being blurred.

One of the liveliest debates in church circles today involves
what is called the "conversion" of the "power structures."
The very expression "power structure" is unfamiliar to many
evangelical ears. It means a government, an army, a corporation, an institution, or any aggregation of influence in a
complex of human relationships. Some churchmen are maintaining that the conversion of the power structures needs to
be emphasized more than the winning of individual men
and women to Jesus Christ. To capture these citadels of
power and influence, according to this line of thinking, is to
take a giant step forward in the securing of peace and justice
for mankind.

It would clarify the debate to examine the term "structure"
more carefully. The application of the word to democratic
institutions is Marxist. Professor Roger Mehl of France
writes, "Marxism . . . discovered that the chief problems of
social ethics are problems of structures. These are objective
realities which evolve in accordance with their own laws. It is
possible to make a scientific study of them. . . . Individual decisions and good will have no power over social structures."[3]
Classically a structure is something built, such as a building,
dam, or bridge. It is solid but inanimate. Used in our present
sense, it is a relatively unstable arrangement of human beings
in some kind of cluster, such as a state government. In this
cluster the components are continually changing. A shift in
control at the top occurs, and policies that were supposed to
be rigid and permanent suddenly change. Whatever else may
be said about a human power structure, it is variable and
unpredictable.

A man, on the other hand, is not a "structure" in the usual
sense, but an organism. Structures go up and are taken
down; a man grows and develops. Capture a man for Christ,
and in the evangelical view as he grows in faith his usefulness
increases. His integrity becomes established and he becomes a

dependable center of influence for good. As the psalmist puts it, he is "like a tree planted by the rivers of water, that bringeth forth his fruit in his season."[4] As the Christian grows in Grace it is not unusual for him to become strategically involved in social relationships, including dealings with governmental power. But instead of becoming one more fluid component of a power bloc, he establishes himself as an independent, self-authenticating base of Christlike influence. He himself affects the government power structure in everything he does. Contrast this radiating witness of a Christian individual with a "converted power structure." In the first place no one really knows how to go about "converting" a power structure apart from the individuals in it. The structure of a state can be radically altered by a political election or a revolution, without any shifting of spiritual values. Change does not imply improvement. All too often new power is not better; it is only different.

When an individual member of society is born of the Spirit of God, the Lord can and does put him to work spreading blessings to those around him. That is because even more than he is seeking to manipulate human structures, the new Christian is reaching out in loving dependence upon the greatest power structure of all—the Trinity! God wants to release his power into the lives of men; and one man with God is a majority. The task facing the church, many evangelicals would say, is not a redefining of evangelism but a more imaginative and creative use of the God-given Biblical concept, using every avenue and approach known to the twentieth-century mind, within the existing authority of a free state.

Conflicts between church and state have taken the lives of thousands of Christian martyrs in the past fifty years. The systematic shooting by Communists of North Korea's pastors during the Korean conflict in 1950-1951 ranked in its severity with the early Roman imperial persecutions.[5] Yet God has not been idle in these turbulent times; revival is still breaking out where men least expect it, in the sovereign activity of the Holy Spirit. A strong evangelistic tide is running in many countries. Occasionally this creates problems, for even under some non-Communist governments a man is not permitted by law to change his religious faith; or else he does so at a tremendous sacrifice.

In many Western countries today there is a minimum of official persecution; yet in the opinion of some there are church-state situations developing that bear watching because of the direction in which they point. One has been created by the sociopolitical penetration of the ecumenical movement. Evangelicals do not all agree about this movement.[6] Some support it, many others oppose it. All would agree that in America ecumenical leadership is exerting considerable pressure upon government agencies. Many look upon the drive toward church union as a bold effort to attain clerical power over the federal government. In this light, the passage of a church resolution on a matter of social and economic policy (such as the Federal Council of Churches statement on labor described in Chapter 5) is considered an intrusion by a church body into matters outside its jurisdiction.

Most evangelicals would say that it is one thing for Christians to express and act on their convictions on public issues; for ministers to explain how they would apply Christian principles to the matters rending the world today; for ministers and laymen to become involved in social, economic, and political problems. But it is quite another thing for a corporate church denomination to speak authoritatively on such issues in the name of all its members. Even here, apparently, the question is not whether the church should ever make public pronouncements on the things that are Caesar's, but how these areas are to be defined and limited.

When an issue is sharply moral, all seem to agree that the church has no choice but to take a stand. (They might disagree as to which stand is the right one.) Evangelicals would be inclined to add that the church should speak only to the moral core of the issue, and not to secular aspects which go beyond its authority and competence.

It is perhaps the genius of democracy that so many folk (Christians among them) act as if they knew what their government should do on every foreign and domestic problem from the Suez Canal to the determination of one-way streets. Such interest in public affairs is normally considered healthy. Whether it is equally healthy to have church denominations acting as pressure groups and political lobbies is not so clear. The history of ecclesiastical intrigue in Western politics makes uneasy reading. Yet the church has a divine mandate to be alert to its social responsibility. One of the first decisions by the New Testament church was the settlement of a social problem, the distribution of food to Greek and Jewish Christians.[7]

In order to stimulate discussion, three suggestions are offered concerning corporate church statements on social matters: First, the pronouncement should deal with the heart of the moral issue and where possible should be couched in general rather than specific terms.[8] Second, the church should make every effort to tidy its own yard by applying the Gospel faithfully to its affairs and problems while it is sharing the Word of Christ with, and proposing solutions to, the world at large.[9] Third, the "official" voice of the churches in public matters might carry far more weight if it were heard more sparingly, and then only on the gravest issues.[10]

POVERTY

The majority of mankind is poor and hungry.[11] The newspapers tell us that every day 10,000 human beings die of starvation or malignant malnutrition, more than in any previous epoch of history; that over half the world's three billion people live in perpetual hunger; that the family pet dog in the United States eats more and better than the average Indian laborer; that Asia has about half the world's population but only one-fourth of the world's food; that in Calcutta 25,000 people have no work and no shelter of any kind, and will live their entire lives on the streets and sidewalks.

The United States Office of Economic Opportunity unearthed some statistics which, while not quite as shocking, are grim enough to prove that there are widespread areas of poverty even in the world's most affluent nation. During the period 1950-1960 many of the world's poorer countries actually lost ground.[12] The 1967 Arab-Israeli war impoverished several nations in the Near East. Flood and famine continue to take their toll in a world that cannot stop fighting long enough to heal its sores.

Evangelist Billy Graham established a healthy precedent in June 1967 when he testified before a Congressional hearing on antipoverty legislation. Dr. Graham read these verses from Deuteronomy 15:7-11:

If there is among you a poor man, one of your brethren, in any of your towns within your land which the Lord your God gives you, you shall not harden your heart or shut your hand against your poor brother, but you shall open your hand to him and lend him sufficient for his need, whatever it may be. Take heed lest there be a base thought in your heart, and you say, "The seventh year, the year of release [of debts] is near," and your eye be hostile to your poor brother, and you give him nothing, and he cry to the Lord against you, and it be sin in you. You shall give to him freely, and your heart shall not be grudging when you give to him, because for this the Lord God will bless you in all your work and in all that you undertake. For the poor will never cease out of the land; therefore I command you, You shall open wide your hand to your brother, to the needy and to the poor, in the land.[13]

For the Christian the "war on poverty" is not a political option. It is a lifelong battle based on the mandate of Jesus Christ, who loved the poor.[14] Young Christians are being called today not only to witness to their Lord, but to conduct the research that will determine whether the earth can supply enough of the basic necessities for existence to meet the demands of expanding population. They are called to help develop industries that will eliminate poverty in backward areas. Vocational opportunities are limited only by the stretch of human imagination and the time of the return of him who said, "Inasmuch as you have done it unto one of the least of these my brethren, you have done it unto me."[15]

HIGHWAY SAFETY

There is probably no place where the average man's religion means less to him than behind the wheel of an automobile. Fifty thousand Americans expire every year in traffic accidents—far more than in combat—yet at this writing not a single evangelical book has appeared, and scarcely an article has been written, on the relationship of Christianity to motor transportation. It seems almost as if many evangelicals feel that the Word of God has nothing to say about driving in traffic and that they are free therefore to interpret the rules of the road as they wish. The New Testament does however have something to say. It says that "the powers that be are ordained of God";[16] and while an ordinary traffic patrolman might object to such ordination, he is nevertheless according to Scripture a servant of the Almighty in the execution of his duty.

Faced with problems of increasing violations, congested courts, mounting insurance claims, and escalating death on the highways, traffic experts are beginning to evolve a kind of doctrine of man-as-motorist.[17] They tell us that the essential cause of accidents is undisciplined human nature; that is, people driving as people (the Bible would say, "Man is prone to sin"). They tell us that drivers do not take kindly to authority; that they do not readily see their driving as needing improvement or correction (the Bible would call them "rebellious hearts" and "stiff necks"). They tell us that accidents are caused when people mix their driving with such attitudes as vanity, selfishness, impatience, exasperation, temper, resentment, inattention, impulsiveness, aggressiveness, competitiveness, indecisiveness, and irresponsibility (the Bible's list of sins is not too different).

Of Jehu, the early Hebrew charioteer, it was said: "He driveth furiously."[18] Of modern drivers the worst practices listed by traffic authorities are "excessive speed into intersections, excessive speed into areas of restricted view, excessive speed under hazardous road conditions, ill-considered passing, wrong-side-of-the-road driving, driving after drinking, inattention to driving, too-close following, driving while greatly fatigued, rushing red and green lights, chiseling on stop signs, changing lanes suddenly without looking or signaling, aggressively asserting right of way, turning from and into incorrect lanes." Attempts to give consistent police attention to these common practices are almost overwhelmed by the actual number of violations.

There are signs that some evangelicals are beginning to be pricked by their social conscience in the matter of highway safety. An organization known as "Transport for Christ" has recently come into being in Canada, and its ministry has spread to the United States. The field of service open to these evangelists is an immense one. While to date their work has been primarily with truck drivers, it is hoped that as "Transport for Christ" grows, the average motorist will not be overlooked.[19]

CAPITAL PUNISHMENT

Clarence Darrow once remarked that in choosing a jury to try one of his defendants, he preferred to seat Unitarians and Methodists and to excuse Lutherans and Presbyterians. The reason, he said, was that the latter two types invariably "voted to convict." Whether the famed lawyer's shrewd observation was true or not, it illustrates the truth that important legal questions such as capital punishment go beyond the courts in their implications. The extreme penalty is hardly an affair limited to the electric chair or the gas chamber. It involves what a person believes about the sanctity and inviolability of human life; the question as to whether a man by his actions ever forfeits the right to live; the moral right (or lack of it) of a society to put a human being to death; and the possibility of life after death.

The evangelical community is divided on the issue of capital punishment, but if a poll were taken it might show that a larger proportion of evangelicals over average citizens would be found unwilling to abolish the death penalty. The position is an unpopular one today and the one who holds it usually prefers to avoid the subject in conversation, since the inference seems to be drawn that there is a cruel and sadistic streak in his nature. The overwhelming opinion of penologists, prison wardens, prison chaplains, jurists, and other authorities has been recorded to the effect that capital punishment does not deter crime.[20] Many killers have testified that at the time of murder, the thought of the death penalty did not impede in the slightest their determination to kill.

The evangelical gives these opinions full weight. He does not deny that in court practice there are serious problems connected with the death penalty: for example, a wealthy white murderer is far less likely to lose his life than a poor Negro murderer. However, when a white man slaughtered eight other persons in cold blood in the state of Illinois in 1966, the trial jury that found him guilty recommended the extreme penalty. Many evangelicals will contend that from the viewpoint of society's protection there was no other choice.

That judgment is based in part on the Old Testament, which condemns murder as contrary to God's will expressed in the sixth commandment. According to the Mosaic code, "the murderer shall surely be put to death."[21] Christians do not consider some strictures of Old Testament law to be binding according to the teaching of Jesus. Yet murder is also condemned in the New Testament.[22] If the issue of "love versus law" be raised, a case can be made for the death penalty on the basis of love—not vengeance, not spite, not retribution, not punishment, not justice, but love in its ultimate sense: love that desires through good laws to provide safety and protection for all the people. Because the enforced legal death of a convicted murderer (of whose identity there is no doubt) has removed a menace to life, certain law-abiding citizens will be enabled to live out their full days. Had he been paroled back to society, they would be dead—murdered.

There are objections to such a view. It could be claimed that it ignores the soul of the murderer himself whom Jesus also died to save. Some of the noblest passages in Scripture tell of mercy rejoicing over justice.[23] Further, many murderers have been reclaimed for humanity and many have been converted to Jesus Christ. Paul himself was once an accessory to a lynching.[24] It is also objected that putting the killer to death does not help society; during the sixteenth century when use of the death penalty was particularly harsh in European countries, crime reigned virtually unchecked.

The author admits his inability to demolish such arguments. Of course the legal death of a criminal is a horrible thing, but the rampant spread of major crime is even more horrible in our time. Criminals are becoming more brazen daily; conditions in the great cities have reached alarming proportions. Many evangelicals who are being goaded into action by the worsening statistics protest that those who would end capital punishment are ignoring psychological factors, of which possibly even the criminals themselves are not aware. Fear is a deep-seated motivator in deflecting the antisocial impulses of human beings. It prevents countless accidents on the highways. Properly used, it impresses restraint on potential criminals. A military leader of the Allied Expeditionary Forces in World War II informed me that he markedly reduced the monthly rate of major crimes committed by his troops upon the French citizenry in Normandy in 1944. He did it by deliberately spreading among his units the fear of capital punishment.[25]

As crimes of violence mount in the West; as more and more armed maniacs roam the city streets, trained expertly to kill, the evangelical believes that society will soon reach a saturation point. It will come to recognize that the elimination of capital punishment may not always be the best thing for the commonweal; and that the wisdom of the Bible is not to be taken lightly.

ABORTION

The question of legalized abortion is now confronting the Western world. In most civilized countries medical ethics and the law permit the deliberate termination of pregnancy, called therapeutic abortion, when the mother's health, life, or reason is clearly jeopardized. In recent years increasing pressure has been applied to lawmaking bodies to authorize abortions to save a pregnant woman from possible serious mental or physical harm, to prevent the birth of a mentally or physically defective child, or to terminate a pregnancy resulting from rape or incest. In religious circles the Roman Catholic Church has taken a strong position against liberalizing the abortion laws. The Roman clergy considers the fetus to be a potential human being, i.e., a person, from the moment of conception. To induce abortion by surgically destroying the fetus is therefore held to be the taking of a human life, in violation of the divine commandment.

Evangelical opinion may differ from the official Roman view in placing more emphasis on the health and well-being of the mother than on the survival of the fetus. However, evangelicals who take the sinfulness of man seriously would hold it an extremely dangerous practice to give to any man, medically trained or not, the power over life and death. They would not oppose some changes in the laws respecting abortion, perhaps (such as have been approved in certain states), but the great need among evangelicals today is for open discussion of the matter. The time for artificial conversational barriers is past. Adult Bible classes should be applying Scripture to the issues. Who decides whether a mother will suffer mental harm from a continued pregnancy? What percentage of defective offspring can be determined in advance? How should a doctor react to a patient who might claim that her pregnancy was incestuous simply in order to obtain a legal abortion? It is to be hoped that the Christian Medical Society will set the pace in enlightened consideration of such questions in the years immediately ahead.[26]

EUTHANASIA

Euthanasia is the act (now illegal in all civilized countries) of painlessly putting to death persons suffering from incurable and distressing disease. Recently strong stands have been taken in Europe and America by intellectual leaders, including some clergymen, in favor of euthanasia. Evangelical opinion on the subject tends to be conservative, not because of a lack of pity for the victims of suffering, but because it is felt the practice of euthanasia would create even graver problems than now exist. As in the case of induced abortion, the basic question becomes: "Who decides when a person is better off dead than alive?" Or to put it another way, "Who accepts the responsibility for the continuation or termination of human life? Who knows at what point the possibility of healing miracle has finally passed?"

The conscientious physician is already sore beset under existing law when he faces a dying patient who begs for a fatal injection that will take him "out of it." To give a doctor the authorization to snuff out life is to hand him more responsibility than any man ought to be asked to bear. It also implies that other men, under other conditions, might be given such authorization. (The Nazi attitude toward mental patients is a living memory.) The object of euthanasia, to be sure, is to bring some relief from the pain in the world. Evangelical Christian doctors and scholars owe it to the churches to help people understand this proposal to introduce a form of mercy into the closing moments of one's existence, and the tremendous difficulties attached to it.

Unnatural Sex

At no point, perhaps, does the evangelical differ from some of his contemporaries more sharply than in his attitude toward unnatural sex practices. To him Paul's description of the body as the temple of the Holy Spirit is literal truth.[27] There is a resistance, therefore, to the new wave of leniency toward sexual deviation. Sometimes this resistance is attributed to a naturally conservative bent, sometimes to Victorianism, legalism, prudishness, personal inhibitions, and even to bad toilet training! Speaking in general terms, none of these causes is the correct one. The core of evangelical refusal to accept sodomy, lesbianism, incest, and all other forms of unnatural sexual vice into Christian society is strictly Biblical.

In his first Letter to the Corinthians Paul writes, according to the Revised Standard Version: "Do not be deceived; neither the immoral, nor idolators, nor adulterers, nor homosexuals, nor thieves, nor the greedy, nor drunkards, nor revilers, nor robbers will inherit the kingdom of God."[28] The Apostle's verdict is an echo of the judgment of God upon Sodom and Gomorrah and the stern warnings of Mosaic law.[29] Sacred prostitution, both male and female, was part of the idolatrous Canaanite worship that the Israelites encountered when they entered Palestine.[30] It was forbidden in Hebrew society in the strongest terms.

The sex obsession that has become such a problem to Western culture has cast a shadow over the pleasant normal relations that have existed for centuries between members of the same sex. Freudian sexual theories have unfortunately contributed to the unhealthy atmosphere. Evil and perverted writers have sought to attribute unnatural relations to David and Jonathan simply because they loved each other.[31] Our Lord himself has not escaped the calumnies of the sex-controlled mind. Pederasts and other advocates of unnatural sexuality have been a powerful force on the stage for several decades of the twentieth century. Their literature has won wide readership in recent years. Lately they have been picketing the White House and pleading their cause on television in their drive to win acceptance into the Armed Forces and in society generally. They are beginning to insist upon the right to adopt children in order to train them in their practices.

Evangelicals admit to a certain amount of loathing where

unnatural sex practices are concerned, but their resistance goes deeper than revulsion. There is evidence that such vices marked the final states of degradation and dissolution in many ancient civilizations besides Sodom and Gomorrah. If Western culture countenances and endorses such habits, and repeals the laws forbidding them, evangelicals believe that it is doomed by the judgment of God to early extinction.

Such a conviction does not affect in the slightest the love in Christ that the Christian has for the sexual deviate. Paul reminded the believers in Corinth that some of them, too, were once such offenders, but that they were now washed, justified, and sanctified by the Lord Jesus Christ.[32] The way of the cross is the same for the homosexual as for the hetero-sexual. The cleansing blood of our Lord is as efficacious for the deviate as it is for the most innocent of human beings. Because of their horror over the business, evangelicals have not often reached out in *agape* (Christian love) to help such people, but have left the work of reclamation to others. Yet the counsel, encouragement, and hope in the Bible are desperately needed by these tortured spirits, many of whom are very young indeed, and are begging for spiritual help. In recent years a new generation of evangelicals is beginning to work in an urban ministry that is touching some of them. There is great need for case studies to be published and circulated, so that such a ministry can be widened and made more effective.

ALCOHOL

The social problems created by the nonindustrial sale and use of alcohol are too vast to be treated in the space allowed. The stand of most evangelicals on the liquor question is all too well known. The permissive attitude of the general pub-lic, regulated by a careful and almost overwhelming program of education conducted by the liquor interests, has reduced the evangelical position to something close to ridicule. Liquor now maintains a powerful interest in, if not control of, the mass media, professional sports, municipal and state politics, and many other normal channels of life.

Prohibition has been deliberately made the whipping boy for every American crime committed between 1918 and 1933. It is a fact that American prohibition was a product in part of the evangelical's social conscience. Whether it was successful is not for this study to decide. The benefits brought by the elimination of alcohol from the scene have never been assessed; only the abuses and ill effects have been recounted *ad infinitum*. Yet they are seldom measured against the havoc that has been wrought in the years since repeal by the billions and billions of gallons of alcohol consumed in the United States. The warp and woof of modern society's pattern of tragedy is drenched in spirits. Behind so many crimes, highway accidents, domestic shipwrecks, and street riots is the specter of John Barleycorn. Alcoholism is more than a medical problem and more than a social problem. It involves ethical and moral issues that can be resolved only by a transformation of character.

The Bible has been greatly abused and misused by those who have sought to use it to defend their position with regard to alcohol. There is actually Biblical warrant for both temperance and moderation. Abstinence has been practiced by millions of the faithful through the centuries who would have it no other way. In other cultures moderation has been a Christian custom. Today's total abstainer unfortunately finds himself a lorn soul when he travels on a jet airplane. But if he is a Christian, he does well to remember that his self-discipline does not honor his Lord or even improve his character, unless it is practiced in love and compassion for the seatmate beside him.

TOBACCO

The churches have fought a losing battle against tobacco for 350 years. Many have given up the struggle and are resigned to filling their parish social rooms with foul air. Their clergy have adopted the cigarette as a symbol of "identification" with life. Many evangelical churches have also muted the discussion of the evils of tobacco simply because of the overwhelming popularity of the habit. Ministers who preach against smoking are singled out as being guilty of nit-picking. People ask, are there not many worse personal habits— marijuana, for example, and LSD, STP, and heroin?

The capitulation of the churches has come about at a time when government health authorities are finally discovering that the use of tobacco is a serious menace to health. The incidence of lung cancer is now so well known that even the highly paid tobacco company doctors can no longer muddy the issue with their "research." The torch of the social conscience dropped by the Christian churches has been picked up by the United States Government and the American Cancer Society, and similar agencies in other countries. Science is now preaching against tobacco with increasing earnestness.

Millions of smokers feel guilty every time they light a cigarette. They know they ought to stop, and they would like to stop, but they are chained by habit, by advertising, and by the absence of good advice on the subject given without moralistic overtones. They need Christ's help. Too many irritated evangelicals are limiting their comments on tobacco to such Biblical quotations as: "Him that is filthy, let him be filthy still."[33] It is certainly true that many tobacco smokers are thoughtless folk, and their ways easily become offensive. But evangelicals need to remember that the Bible's word to smokers is the same as it is to nonsmokers: "Look unto me and be saved, all the ends of the earth."[34]

Chapter 14

The Horse and the Cart

Great changes do not begin on the surface of society, but in prepared hearts: in men who by communion with God, rise above the apathy of the age, and speak with living vital energy, and give life to the community, and tone to the public mind.

—Edward Beecher

In God's creation man stands paramount. "Thou madest him to have dominion over the works of thy hands; thou hast put all things under his feet."[1] The reflective capacity of the human mind and the strength of the human will are beyond all the powers of nature to match. As Pico della Mirandola wrote in the days of the Renaissance, man is the most marvelous thing ever seen upon the stage of the world.[2] Because man was made in the image and likeness of God, no attempt to ridicule or belittle him can ultimately succeed; when Harry Elmer Barnes asserted that "astronomically speaking, man is insignificant," George A. Coe replied, "Astronomically speaking, man is the astronomer."[3]

Yet according to the Bible this masterpiece of all creation, man, rebelled against the One who made him. In his Promethean pride he defied the Supreme Power of the universe and attempted to take the regulation of existence into his own hands. In so doing man severed the silken strands that linked him to his Heavenly Father's purpose for his life. The evangelical looks at history as the tragic unfolding of events after human aspiration supplanted the divine plan and left man without an invisible means of support. Pride, fear, greed, lust, deceit, callousness, vindictiveness, took over the role of supplying human motivation and largely dictated human behavior.

Today, surrounded by the artifacts of his brilliant competence, man stands in ruins. He has cut God out of his life, and his life has accordingly lost its meaning; as Christoph Blumhardt once said, "Our life has no meaning in itself; it has meaning only in relation to God."[4] The present cult of universal "unmeaning" as propounded by existentialist philosophers is to the Christian merely a reflection upon the homelessness of man as sinner. It contains nothing new. A "meaningless" universe is not the logical deduction of natural science, but the bold invention of natural man; that is, of man in insurrection against God. Aldous Huxley once wrote, "I had motives for not wanting the world to have a meaning; consequently assumed that it had none; and was able without any difficulty to find gratifying reasons for this assumption. Those who detect no meaning in the world generally do so because, for one reason or another, it suits their books that the world should be meaningless. We objected to the morality because it interfered with our sexual freedom."[5]

The evangelical Christian believes with all his soul that his Lord has put meaning and purpose into the created order; that God is not the author of confusion.[6] His own efforts to flex his social conscience in the latter twentieth century are not a wild striking out against the blind cruelties of a dastardly fate. The foregoing chapters have all sought to show that for a Christian to put his social conscience to work is to assert the true manhood that was destroyed by sin but restored in Jesus Christ. After all, the greatest fact about man is not that he can laugh or pray or handle tools or go touring in space; the greatest fact about him is that God loves him in Jesus Christ. When a convert has "put on the new man" in Christ he starts putting legs under the compassion that God has sensitized. All the potential given to the original Adam, and lost, is now his again, because he is living in obedience as God intended him to live—not for himself but for his fellow. He looks at his fellow man in his magnificent misery through the eyes of Christ. He seeks to apply the redeeming Spirit of Christ to the hidden springs of man's behavior, to the seat of motivation and activation that is known in God's Word as the "heart." "I should give a false impression of my own convictions," said William Temple, "if I did not [state] that there is no hope of establishing a more Christian social order except through the labor and sacrifice of those in whom the Spirit of Christ is active."[7]

In the evangelical view, the church is called of God to announce the glad tidings of God's love, the gift of salvation freely offered to all. It is commissioned to bring men and nations under the preaching of the cross; to declare the holiness and righteousness of God, and the sinfulness of men; to warn of eternal judgment to come; and to point to the Man Christ Jesus as the atoning Lord of love and the one hope for a lost world. Christians are considered in the New Testament a peculiar people set apart to proclaim that message to individuals, to groups, to races, to peoples everywhere. They have been entrusted with a Word of Grace and compassion, redemption and reconciliation, liberation and sanctifying power. The church accordingly is functioning correctly when it faces every man born into the world with his need to be reborn in Jesus Christ—including every reader of this book. God has a plan; that plan is Christ, and the sooner men recognize him, turn from their sins, and receive and acknowledge Christ as Savior and Lord, the sooner they enter his Kingdom.

To say all this without love, however, is worse than useless; it is demonic. Christianity is not a religion but a relationship of love expressed toward God and men. The church is committed by its Founder to reach out in love to every movement that upbuilds character and integrity in men, and every gesture that aims to resolve the differences that estrange human beings from each other. The Gospel in its free course goes hand in hand with the cup of cold water.

If some Christians seem slow to grasp the social implications of the evangel in a day of mass communication, that disparity is not going unnoticed. Within evangelicalism men are beginning to voice their concern over the credibility gap in the evangelical's social conscience. They would like to see the distance closed between words and deeds, theory and practice. They would like to see the new man in Christ behaving more like Jesus of Nazareth, who even in his highest moments of prayer never forgot people. They would like to see the whole relationship of the Gospel to society reexamined.

One of the more representative expressions of this concern was delivered by Dr. Horace L. Fenton, Jr., general director of the Latin America Mission, at the Wheaton, Illinois "Congress on the Church's Worldwide Mission" in 1966. Dr. Fenton declared,

Many evangelicals seem to have concluded that while compassion and charity are certainly an important part of our message, this does not imply a deep sense of social responsibility on the part of the church. Fortunately, they do not tell the whole story. Other evangelicals today show a changed attitude toward these matters and recognize the importance of social concern as a manifestation of their obedience to Christ.

What accounts for this change? For one thing, a careful reexamination of the scriptural teaching on the subject has led many evangelicals to feel that they have been unconsciously overlooking certain Biblical emphases. There seem to be whole areas, not only in the Old Testament prophets, with their demands for social justice, but also in the teachings of Christ and the apostles, to which we have given too little heed. Some of the best-loved parables of our Lord have not had their full impact on us, and the example of his earthly life still has much to say to us. Indeed, a study of our Lord's earthly life clearly teaches us that, while he majored on the spiritual and the eternal, he never minimized or ignored the physical needs of men.

There is abundant precedent in church history, ancient and modern, for a much closer connection between the preaching of the Gospel and social concern than we have often allowed. We are also learning that, while the faithful preaching of the Gospel has social effects, these results do not necessarily follow as an inevitable, automatic consequence. Any individual, as a member of humanity, has certain responsibilities to society. The Biblical writers bear witness to the fact that his new life needs to be channeled into avenues of service which are fruitful for Christ and beneficial for his fellow men.

If the church shirks her duty to show the application of the Christian faith to the social needs of men, she does it at the expense of the good name of Christ in the world. It is all too possible for an individual believer to fail to see the connection between his love for God and his responsibility to his fellow men, unless it is pointed out to him—not just once, but many times. To expect the Holy Spirit to do this, apart from the church, which is his chosen instrument, is a hope which finds no basis in either Scripture or Christian experience.

There is an increasing awareness on the part of evangelicals that the relationship of mission and social concern is made doubly important by the revolutionary nature of the times in which we live. If, by our lack of social concern, we bring opprobrium upon the evangelical message, we shall have only ourselves to blame for the fact that we cannot get an audience. And we shall answer to God for the inadequate and inaccurate way in which we have represented him. In our own day, we know better than ever that a man's social context has a bearing on his receptivity to the Gospel, and that, consequently, social concern is and must be an integral part of all true evangelism.

Any evangelism which ignores social concern is by its nature an incomplete and unscriptural evangelism, and it will likely end up by being an unheeded evangelism. . . . Are there any principles that will help us?

In the first place, any program of social action which is a part of mission must point men to—not away from—the central message of redemption through the blood of Christ.

Second, our expression of social concern must provide, wherever possible, for a spoken witness to Christ. Because we desire the best for the ones to whom we minister, we long that our expression of social concern shall be an introduction to Jesus Christ, who can meet their needs in a way and to an extent never possible to us.

Third, we must make sure that our efforts do not arouse idealistic and unscriptural expectations. We identify ourselves gladly, as servants of Christ, with the struggles for a just social order, at the same time remembering—and pointing out—the fact that man's highest hopes in this realm will be realized, not through any man-made institution, but only by Christ at his coming. We do not refuse man help in his social situation on the grounds that his problems are basically spiritual, but we dare not allow him to forget that any explanation of man's social ills which overlooks his broken relationship with God is superficial and inadequate.

Fourth, we need to remember that our desire to do good in the name of Christ should not lead us into wasteful competition with secular agencies.

We have, as evangelicals, something unique to bring to the realm of mission and social concern, a motivation and a dynamic which men outside of Christ, however humanitarian they may be, cannot experience. Yet what we have done so far has almost always been too little, and often it has been too late. There are, to be sure, many unanswered questions, many unsolved problems in this realm of mission and social concern. But there are great rewards, too, here and hereafter. And the price of failure, brought about by presenting an incomplete, irrelevant Gospel, is *very* high[8] [italics the speaker's].

Dr. Fenton's statements summarize what can be called the burden of this book: that judgment must begin at the house of God.[9] Today's evangelicals cannot pretend to a superior nobility of character, or a tenderer social compassion, or a vaster knowledge of metaphysics; nor can they use any other yardstick by which men grade themselves above their fellows. At the same time they are not necessarily worse than other men, more callous to human need or more hypocritical in in their attitudes and behavior. What is important for the record is that many of them are now dissatisfied with what has been done and left undone in their relations with society, and they intend to spend the rest of the twentieth century amending and balancing the account.[10]

The issue inevitably reverts to the Book, for the evangelical (whatever else he may be) is a man of the Book. He looks upon the Bible as the Word of God, and draws upon it daily for strength. In the Old and New Testaments he has found the way to Heaven, with the equipment and stores to get him there. He will also find, if he looks closer, clear and definite guidance in the pages of Scripture for the social behavior of the believer:

See that your public behavior is above criticism. As far as your responsibility goes, live at peace with everyone. Do good to all men as opportunity offers. Have a reputation for gentleness. May the Lord give you increasing love . . . toward all men. Be very patient with all men. Good should be your objective always . . . in the world at large. Be kind to all. Let it be your ambition to live at peace with all men. Honor all men. For we are his workmanship, created in Christ Jesus for good works, which God prepared beforehand, that we should walk in them. I desire you to insist on these things, so that those who have believed in God may be careful to apply themselves to good deeds; these are excellent and profitable to men.[11]

There is no way to circumvent these statements. They create their own moral authority, and they leave the Christian no doubt as to what his position is to be with regard to the human race. Perhaps it is time for evangelicals to withdraw from the sterile debate as to who is putting the cart before the horse. There will always be those in the world who claim that beliefs condition behavior; and there will always be those who say that it does not matter what a person believes, so long as his actions are socially acceptable. The issue cannot in any case be settled by argument; and the people of the Book would look far better if they simply left the question of priorities to work itself out, and they in turn got about the King's business.

James was not wrong when he demanded that Christians show their faith by their works.[12] Jesus Christ was not wrong when he told his listeners in effect to stop sitting on their hands and to get to work doing God's will.[13] He did not come to earth to split theological hairs, but to minister to a world of need and to save men out of it for eternity. It is time the air was cleared. To pit social action against evangelism is to raise a phony issue, one that Jesus would have spiked in a sentence. He commanded his disciples to spread the Good News, and to let their social concern be made manifest through the changed lives of persons of ultimate worth. Today that command is as much needed as it was in primitive Palestine, but there is a fresh eschatological imperative added: the time is short. As Billy Graham warns, we are traveling on a collision course, and ahead of us looms catastrophe.

Let the evangelical then recommit his life to God and gird his loins. Looking no longer at the evil behind him, and not eyeing too closely the neighbor alongside him, let him pull his own weight and some to spare. And as God gives opportunity, let him be a friend to his neighbor as well as a helper, and share with him the good things of Christ. *Even so come, Lord Jesus.*

Notes

CHAPTER 1

1. In *Primer for Protestants* (New York: Association Press, 1951), p. 34.
2. In an interview with the author in Zürich, Switzerland, June 1950.
3. Amos 9:7.
4. Acts 9:17; 22:12-13.
5. John Masefield, "The Everlasting Mercy," in *Poems* (New York: The Macmillan Co., 1945).
6. 2 Corinthians 10:4.

CHAPTER 2

1. 1 Corinthians 3:22-23 (RSV).
2. James 2:14-16 (Phillips).
3. Exodus 5:1.
4. Amos 5:24 (RSV).
5. Isaiah 3:15 (RSV).
6. Hosea 4:1-2 (RSV).
7. Micah 7:2 (RSV).
8. Jeremiah 22:3 (RSV).
9. Ezekiel 18:25, 32 (RSV).
10. Leviticus 25.
11. *Cambridge Ancient History* (London: Cambridge University Press, 1952), Vol. 10, p. 705.
12. Stanley G. Evans, *The Social Hope of the Church* (London: Hodder & Stoughton, 1965), p. 17.
13. *Ibid.*, p. 19.
14. Psalm 146:5-9.
15. John 3:16.
16. Evans, *op. cit.*, pp. 37-38.
17. Exposition of Luke by Dr. H. D. M. Spence in *The Pulpit Commentary* (Grand Rapids, Mich.: Eerdmans Publishing Co., 1958), Vol. 16, p. 10.
18. Luke 1:51-53 (RSV).
19. Josephus, *Wars of the Jews*, Book 2, Chap. 5.
20. Luke 1:54-55 (RSV).
21. John 2:4.
22. Luke 3:14.
23. Luke 2:19.
24. Edward Gibbon, *Decline and Fall of the Roman Empire* (New York: Peter Fenelon Collier, 1899), Vol. 1, p. 65.
25. See pp. 23, 65-66.
26. *Cambridge Ancient History* (London: Cambridge University Press, 1951), Vol. 9, pp. 787, 875.
27. Cf. the resistance and persecution of Wang Ming-tao in Leslie Lyall, *Come Wind, Come Weather* (Chicago: Moody Press, 1960), pp. 38-51; see also *Decision* magazine, October 1967.

28. Galatians 3:28.

29. Herbert Butterfield, *Christianity and History* (London: G. Bell & Sons, 1949), pp. 134-35.

30. Ernst Troeltsch, *The Social Teaching of the Christian Churches,* Olive Wyon, trans. (New York: The Macmillan Co.; London: Allen & Unwin, 1931), Vol. 1, p. 62.

CHAPTER 3

1. John 10:10.

2. John 7:37 (RSV).

3. Isaiah 53:5.

4. What Bonhoeffer said was that he looked upon Jesus as "one whose only concern is for others . . . . man existing for others, and hence the Crucified." From notes for the outline of a book (tr.) in the *Chicago Theological Seminary Register,* Vol. 51 (February 1961). Quoted by J. A. T. Robinson in *Honest to God* (Philadelphia: Westminster Press; London: SCM Press, 1963), p. 76.

5. John 16:7 (Phillips).

6. Troeltsch, *op. cit.,* Vol. 1, p. 61.

7. Mark 12:40.

8. Mark 7:11.

9. Matthew 7:21 (RSV).

10. John 15:13.

11. Matthew 12:12 (RSV).

12. Luke 13:32.

13. Luke 12:14.

14. Mark 10:43-45.

15. Matthew 5:13-14.

16. John 15.

17. Matthew 5:44.

18. Matthew 23:4.

19. Matthew 2:27-28.

20. Karl Barth, *Epistle to the Romans,* Edwyn C. Hoskyns, trans. (London: Oxford University Press, 1932), pp. 330-423.

21. Lenin expressed a similar view. Cf. Alexander Miller, *The Christian Significance of Karl Marx* (London: SCM Press, 1946), p. 40.

22. 1 Samuel 21:6.

CHAPTER 4

Opening quotation by Bishop Warburton from Walter Russell Bowie, *Which Way Ahead?* (New York: Harper & Brothers, 1943), p. 46.

1. Charles Williams, *The Descent of the Dove* (New York: Pellegrini & Cudahy, 1939), pp. 107-08.

2. From Helen H. Harris, *The Newly Recovered Apology of Aristides* (London: Hodder & Stoughton, 1893); see also *Decision* magazine, June 1967.

3. *Ante-Nicene Fathers* (American ed.; Grand Rapids, Mich.: Eerdmans Publishing Co.), Vol. 1, pp. 26-27.

NOTES   159

4. Mark 2:27 (RSV).
5. G. S. M. Walker, *The Growing Storm* (Grand Rapids, Mich.: Eerdmans Publishing Co.; London: Paternoster Press, 1961), p. 174.
6. C. Loring Brace, *Gesta Christi* (London: Hodder & Stoughton, 1884), pp. 84-223.
7. Johannes Tauler, *Die Predigten Taulers*, F. Vetter, ed. (Berlin, 1910), pp. 13-14, 240-43.
8. Walker, *op. cit.*, p. 210.
9. Jean Rilliet, *Zwingli, Third Man of the Reformation*, Harold Knight, trans. (Philadelphia: Westminster Press, 1964), pp. 89-91.
10. Samuel Eliot Morison, *Builders of the Bay Colony* (New York: Houghton Mifflin Co., 1930), pp. 289-319.
11. Henry K. Rowe, *Modern Pathfinders of Christianity* (New York: Fleming H. Revell, 1928), pp. 137-49.
12. Following is the text of Wesley's letter, taken from *The Life of William Wilberforce*, by his sons, Robert and Samuel (Philadelphia: Henry Perkins, 1839), p. 99:

MY DEAR SIR,

Unless the Divine power has raised you up to be as Athanasius *contra mundum*, I see not how you can go through your glorious enterprise, in opposing that execrable villany which is the scandal of religion, of England, and of human nature. Unless God has raised you up for this very thing, you will be worn out by the opposition of men and devils; but if God be for you who can be against you. Are all of them together stronger than God? Oh be not weary of well doing. Go on in the name of God, and in the power of his might, till even American slavery, the vilest that ever saw the sun, shall vanish away before it. That he who has guided you from your youth up may continue to strengthen you in this and all things, is the prayer of,

Dear Sir,
Your affectionate servant,

JOHN WESLEY
February 24, 1791

13. *Ibid.*, p. 528.
14. Butterfield, *Christianity and History*, p. 134.
15. G. A. Best, *Shaftesbury* (London: B. T. Batsford, 1964), p. 111.

CHAPTER 5

1. Lewis Mumford, *Technics and Civilization* (London: G. Routledge Sons, 1946), p. 359.
2. Mark 2:27.
3. M. S. Viteles, *The Science of Work* (New York: W. W. Norton & Co., 1934), p. 369.
4. Henri De Man, *Joy in Work*, Eden and Cedar Paul, trans. (London: Allen & Unwin, 1929), p. 50.
5. See pp. 32-36.
6. The most detailed description of the movement is still C. H. Hopkins'

work, *The Rise of the Social Gospel in American Protestantism, 1865-1915* (New Haven: Yale University Press, 1940).

7. Timothy Smith, *Revivalism and Social Reform* (Nashville, Tenn.: Abingdon Press, 1957); see especially pp. 148-62.

8. Cf. the five sermons delivered by the Rev. Edward Beecher, president of Illinois College, published in *The American National Preacher*, June and July 1835, on the subject, "The Nature, Importance, and Means of Eminent Holiness Throughout the Church."

9. See pp. 34-35.

10. Smith, *op. cit.*, p. 180.

11. They included such well-known pulpit figures as Washington Gladden, Graham Taylor, Stephen Peabody, and Walter Rauschenbusch, among others.

12. The expression is Dorothy Sayers' and is found in *Creed or Chaos* (London: Methuen & Co.; New York: Harcourt, Brace & World, 1947), p. 58.

13. Walter Rauschenbusch, *A Theology for the Social Gospel* (New York: The Macmillan Co., 1918), p. 35.

14. The statement may be found in Harry F. Ward, *The Social Creed of the Churches* (New York: Eaton & Mains, 1914), p. 7.

15. See pp. 133-34.

16. *Sam Jones' and Sam Small's Sermons* (Chicago: Geo. W. Ogilvie, 1890), p. 6.

17. For an interesting critique by a non-Christian, see Gertrude Himmelfarb, *Darwin and the Darwinian Revolution* (Garden City, L.I.: Doubleday & Co., 1959).

CHAPTER 6

1. Carl F. H. Henry, *The Uneasy Conscience of Modern Fundamentalism* (Grand Rapids, Mich.: Eerdmans Publishing Co., 1947), pp. 23, 26.

2. *Ibid.*, p. 84.

3. Special mention should be made of the pioneering and socially significant work done on the European continent by Spener and Francke at Halle, Fliedner at Kaiserswerth, the Blumhardts at Bad Boll, and the activities of the "inner missions" in Denmark and Germany.

4. Isaiah 58:6-7 (RSV).

5. Amos 7:8; 5:12 (RSV).

6. James 2:3-4.

7. *The Church's Worldwide Mission*, Harold Lindsell, ed. (Waco, Texas: Word Books, 1966), pp. 219-20.

8. *Ibid.*, pp. 234-35.

CHAPTER 7

1. W. G. Symons, *Work and Vocation* (London: SCM Press, 1946), p. 13.

2. Thus Rollo May reports one of his clients, a missionary teacher, as confessing to him, "Once some pupils told me in confidence that they knew we teachers were not out in Egypt because we cared about them, the natives, but because of our own beliefs that we ought to serve somebody. I could

not help seeing that this was partly true. . . . The boys saw through our shell. The idea had got around that when we teachers talked about love, it was not Christian love for the natives at all, but love for our own ideal of love" (*The Springs of Creative Living* [Nashville, Tenn.: Abingdon-Cokesbury, 1940], pp. 46-47).

3. Ecclesiastes 3:7 (Moffatt).

4. Revelation 9:3, 7.

5. "Man goeth forth unto his work and to his labor until the evening" (Psalm 104:23).

6. "Listen! The wages of the field hands who harvested your crops, which you have deliberately withheld, screams to heaven; and the cries of exploited harvesters have penetrated the hearing of the Lord of hosts" (James 5:4).

7. Romans 3:22-23.

8. David Lowe, *From Pit to Parliament* (London: Labour Publishing Co., 1923), p. 75.

9. "To speak of the social significance of Holy Communion is no longer novel. . . . The great Community problem of our modern world is how to share bread" (G. F. MacLeod, *Only One Way Left* [Glasgow: Iona Community, 1954], p. 112).

10. D. H. Lawrence, *Pansies* (London: Martin Secker, 1929).

11. Interview in Zürich, Switzerland, June 1950.

12. William Temple, *Nature, Man and God* (London: Macmillan & Co., 1949), p. 408.

13. Cf. W. R. Forrester, *Christian Vocation* (London: Lutterworth Press, 1945), pp. 57-66.

14. N. H. G. Robinson, "The Place of Vocation in Christian Ethics," *Theology* (May 1950), pp. 172-78; also letter to the author, October 3, 1966.

15. Matthew 5:16.

16. John 21:6.

17. See Chap. 5.

18. Proverbs 20:27.

CHAPTER 8

Opening quotation from H. G. Plum, *Restoration Puritanism* (Chapel Hill, N. C.: University of North Carolina Press, 1943), p. 10.

1. Leviticus 25:10.

2. See p. 10.

3. Luke 4:18; Isaiah 61:1 (RSV).

4. George MacMunn, *Slavery Through the Ages* (London: Nicholson & Watson, 1938), p. 6.

5. *The Iliad of Homer,* Samuel Butler, trans., "Great Books of the Western World" (Chicago: University of Chicago, William Benton; Encyclopedia Britannica, 1952), Book XXIV, 752 (p. 179), Book VI, 427 (p. 44).

6. Luke 4:21 (RSV).

7. John 8:32.

8. 2 Corinthians 3:17.

9. James 1:25.

10. 1 Peter 2:16 (RSV).

11. Romans 8:21.

12. Joseph R. Washington, Jr., *The Politics of God* (Boston: Beacon Press, 1967), pp. 109-14.

13. Elton Trueblood, *Foundations for Reconstruction* (New York: Harper & Brothers, 1946), p. 105. Cf. Richard Hooker's words at the end of the sixteenth century: "Laws politic . . . are never framed as they should be, unless presuming the will of man to be inwardly obstinate, rebellious, and averse from all obedience unto the sacred laws of his nature" (*Laws*, I, x, i).

14. *Papers of James Madison*, H. D. Gilpin, ed., Vol. 2, p. 1073. Quoted in Reinhold Niebuhr, *Moral Man and Immoral Society* (New York: Charles Scribner's Sons, 1932), p. 164.

15. Quoted in A. M. Davies, *Foundation of American Freedom* (Nashville, Tenn.: Abingdon Press, 1955), p. 66.

16. John Stuart Mill in *Representative Government*, "Great Books of the Western World" (Chicago: University of Chicago, William Benton; Encyclopedia Britannica, 1952), p. 388.

17. Douglas Campbell, *The Puritan in Holland, England, and America* (New York: Harper & Brothers, 1892), Vol. 2, p. 10.

18. C. S. Lewis, *The Weight of Glory* (New York: The Macmillan Co.; London: Geoffrey Bles, 1949), pp. 36-38.

19. George Leon Walker, *Thomas Hooker* (New York: Dodd, Mead & Co., 1891), p. 125.

20. Alexander Johnston, *Connecticut*, p. 72. Quoted *ibid.*, pp. 127-28.

21. Nathan H. Chamberlain, *Samuel Sewall and the World He Lived In* (Boston: De Wolfe, Fiske & Co., 1897), pp. 15-16.

22. Galatians 2:20 (RSV).

23. G. F. MacLeod, *We Shall Re-build* (Glasgow: Iona Community, 1947), p. 62.

24. Helmut Thielicke, *How the World Began*, J. W. Doberstein, trans. (Philadelphia: Muhlenberg Press, 1961), p. 215.

25. 1 Corinthians 10:27-29.

26. The source of this quotation has been mislaid.

CHAPTER 9

Opening quotation from Chamberlain, *Samuel Sewall, op. cit.*, p. 134.

1. 1 Timothy 2:4 (RSV).

2. Romans 3:22.

3. Romans 5:18.

4. John 1:12.

5. Psalm 147:10.

6. Billy Graham, "God and the Color of a Man's Skin," in *Decision* magazine (August 1965).

7. Acts 17:26.

8. Galatians 5:22.

9. 1 John 4:19.

10. Matthew 25:31-46.

11. The injunctions in the Old Testament against marrying "foreign" wives (e.g., Ezra 10:2, 10) are directed to the issue of belief vs. unbelief, as are

Paul's remarks to the Corinthian Christians (2 Corinthians 6:14). They are based upon spiritual rather than biological considerations. That Moses married an Ethiopian wife appears beyond dispute (Numbers 12:1 ff.).

12. John 8:36.

13. Isaiah 1:16-17 (RSV).

14. Isaiah 55:1.

15. A transcript of the telecast was kindly furnished the author by Station WBAL-TV, Baltimore, Maryland.

CHAPTER 10

1. Genesis 1:10.

2. John 1:12.

3. Ephesians 2:10.

4. Galatians 5:25.

5. The reference is to Alfred C. Kinsey *et al.*, *Sexual Behavior in the Human Male* (Philadelphia: W. B. Saunders, 1948).

6. Elmer G. Homrighausen, "The Church in the World," *Theology Today* (July 1965), pp. 267-69.

7. Justice Klein's opinion is reflected in many recent decisions handed down by British and American courts. According to Scripture when historic standards of decency no longer apply to a people, that people is already under divine judgment (Romans 1:24, 26, 28).

8. Cf. an address given by Justice Oliver Wendell Holmes on January 8, 1897, "The Path of the Law," published in *Harvard Law Review*, Vol. X, pp. 460-61, May 25, 1897: "The prophesies of what the courts will do in fact, and nothing more pretentious, are what I mean by the law." (The author is indebted to Mr. Lawrence E. Nerheim for this citation.)

9. J. A. T. Robinson, *Honest to God*, p. 115.

10. Joseph Fletcher, *Situation Ethics* (Philadelphia: Westminster Press; London: SCM Press, 1966), p. 65.

11. Kant wrote: "Two things fill the mind with ever-increasing wonder and awe, the more often and the more intensely the mind of thought is drawn to them: the starry heavens above me and the moral law within me" (*Critique of Practical Reason*).

12. James Russell Lowell, motto of the American Copyright League, adopted November 20, 1885.

13. Joshua 2:1 ff.

14. Luke 16:1-9.

15. Homrighausen, *op. cit.*, p. 269.

16. Editorial in *Christian Century*, April 13, 1966, pp. 451-52.

17. 1 Corinthians 13:1-3.

18. Fletcher, *op. cit.*, pp. 65, 71, 101.

19. N. H. G. Robinson, *op. cit.*, pp. 172-78; letter to the author, October 3, 1966.

20. The expression is Joseph Sittler's.

21. "Conversations with McLuhan," by Gerald Emanuel Stearn in *Encounter* magazine, London, England (June 1967), p. 56, © 1967 by Gerald Emanuel Stearn and Marshall McLuhan.

22. Nicolas Berdyaev, *The Destiny of Man*, Natalie Duddington, trans. (London: Geoffrey Bles, 1937), p. 144.

CHAPTER 11

1. Nevil Shute, *On the Beach* (New York: William Morrow & Co., 1957), p. 309.
2. Psalm 65:9.
3. Numbers 35:34.
4. Isaiah 24:5.
5. Deuteronomy 28:15-24 (RSV).
6. Alan Paton, *Cry, the Beloved Country* (New York: Charles Scribner's Sons; London: Jonathan Cape, 1948), p. 3.
7. Luke 15:13; 16:1.
8. Luke 12:48 (RSV).
9. Senator Nelson confirmed his statements made on television in a letter to the author, September 23, 1966.
10. Marya Mannes, *More in Anger* (Philadelphia: J. B. Lippincott, 1958), pp. 40-41.
11. S. P. R. Charter, *Man on Earth* (Sausalito, Calif.: Contact Editions, Angel Island Publications, 1962), pp. 47-48.
12. See Note 9, above.
13. Romans 8:21 (RSV).
14. Evans, *Social Hope of the Church, op. cit.*, p. 282.
15. Quoted *ibid.*, p. 282.

CHAPTER 12

1. Mark 13:7-8.
2. James 4:1-2 (RSV).
3. Isaiah 52:7.
4. Mark 9:50 (RSV).
5. Matthew 5:9 (RSV).
6. Isaiah 45:5, 7.
7. Jeremiah 6:14.
8. John Stuart Mill, "The Contest in America," *Fraser's Magazine* (February 1862). Reprinted in *Dissertations and Discussions*, Vol. 3, and quoted in Michael St. John Packe, *The Life of John Stuart Mill* (New York: The Macmillan Co., 1954), p. 424.
9. Editorial in *Christian Century*, September 15, 1965, pp. 1115-16.
10. Says Berdyaev (*Destiny of Man, op. cit.*, p. 256): "Pacifism is the opposite of militarism, but there is no final truth in either. Pacifism is optimistic and ignores the tragic nature of history. There is a certain amount of truth in it—the will, namely, that wars should cease. But pacifism does not recognize the spiritual conditions needed to end wars; it remains . . . unconscious of the irrational forces at work in the world." The pacifist opacity to facts is illustrated by an incident occurring 100 years ago. A group of English pacifists took issue with their government's decision to send its gunboats into action on the high seas. The peace-lovers duly registered a protest. But what

did the government propose to do with its gunboats? It proposed to halt ships that were plying an illegal slave traffic between Africa and the British colonies in the West Indies! (Francis T. McConnell, *Evangelicals, Revolutionists and Idealists* (Nashville, Tenn.: Abingdon Press, 1942), p. 175.

11. Zechariah 4:6.

12. Rudyard Kipling, "Recessional."

13. Berdyaev, *op. cit.*, p. 281.

14. Cf. the moving testimony of Lt.-Gen. Sir William Dobbie, commander of Malta in World War II, in *A Very Present Help* (Grand Rapids, Mich.: Zondervan Publishing Co., 1945), pp. 1-13, 99-121.

15. Ephesians 6:15.

CHAPTER 13

Opening quotation by Edna St. Vincent Millay from "The Anguish," in *Collected Poems* (Harper & Row, 1955).

1. Matthew 5:45.

2. "Evangelicals are not the only Christians. There are those who share with us a firm belief in historic, supernatural Christianity, who worship Christ as Lord and Savior, who take a high view of Scripture, yet who may not use all our terminology and who hold a view of the church and the ministry different from ours. They too are Christians; and from some of them we have much to learn."—Dr. Frank E. Gaebelein, addressing the School of Christian Writing, Minneapolis, Minn., June 18, 1967.

3. In "The Basis of Christian Social Ethics," in *Christian Social Ethics in a Changing World*, John C. Bennett, ed. (New York: Association Press, 1966), pp. 44-45.

4. Psalm 1:3.

5. Cf. Arch Campbell, *The Christ of the Korean Heart* (Columbus, Ohio: Falco Publishers, 1954).

6. Cf. the frequent letters appearing on the subject in the evangelical fortnightly *Christianity Today*.

7. Acts 6:1 ff.

8. Cf. Matthew 5-7.

9. 1 Peter 4:17.

10. Luke 12:14.

11. Edward Rogers, *Poverty on a Small Planet* (New York: The Macmillan Co., 1965), p. 21.

12. *Ibid.*, p. 65.

13. RSV.

14. Luke 6:20.

15. Matthew 25:40.

16. Romans 13:1.

17. From material prepared by Joseph Shields, supervisor of driver education, for the Metropolitan Safety Council of Minnesota. Used by permission.

18. 2 Kings 9:20.

19. Information about "Transport for Christ" may be obtained from 35 Barrhead Crescent, Box 371, Rexdale, Toronto, Canada.

20. Cf. Byron Eshleman, *Death Row Chaplain* (Englewood Cliffs, N. J.: Prentice-Hall, 1962).

21. Numbers 35:16.

22. Matthew 19:18; Mark 7:21; 1 Peter 4:15; 1 John 3:15.

23. E.g., James 2:13.

24. Acts 8:1.

25. This "off the record" information cannot be further documented.

26. Information about the Christian Medical Society may be obtained from 1122 Westgate North, Oak Park, Illinois 60301.

27. 1 Corinthians 3:16.

28. 1 Corinthians 6:9 (RSV).

29. Genesis 19:24; Deuteronomy 23:17.

30. *Harper Study Bible,* Harold Lindsell, ed. (New York: Harper & Row, 1964), p. 287 notes. By permission of Zondervan Publishing Co., Grand Rapids, Michigan.

31. 2 Samuel 1:26.

32. 1 Corinthians 6:11.

33. Revelation 22:11.

34. Isaiah 45:22.

CHAPTER 14

Opening quotation by Edward Beecher from "The Nature, Importance, and Means of Eminent Holiness Throughout the Church," in *The American National Preacher,* X (1835), p. 223.

1. Psalm 8:6.

2. This quotation is found in Zwingli's Sermon on the Providence of God, preached August 30, 1530. It appears in English translation in the Latin works of Huldreich Zwingli, Samuel Macauley Jackson, trans., and W. J. Hinke, ed. (Philadelphia: Heidelberg Press, 1922), Vol. 2, pp. 159 ff. Zwingli attributes it to "Abdullah the Mohammedan." A footnote quotes Pico's oration on the dignity of man as beginning, "I have read, Most Reverend Fathers, in the monuments of the Arabs, that Abdalla, the Sarracen, having been asked what could be seen on this earthly stage that was most to be wondered at, answered that nothing could be seen more wonderful than man." Documentation of this exchange (about the year 1930) is lacking.

4. R. Lejeune, *Christoph Blumhardt and His Message* (Rifton, N. Y.: Plough Publishing House, 1963), p. 152.

5. The source of this quotation has been mislaid.

6. 1 Corinthians 14:33.

7. William Temple, *Christianity and Social Order* (London: Penguin Books, 1942), p. 100.

8. In Lindsell, ed., *Church's Worldwide Mission, op. cit.,* pp. 193-202. Dr. Fenton follows David O. Moberg (*Inasmuch: Christian Social Responsibility in the Twentieth Century* [Grand Rapids, Mich.: Eerdmans Publishing Co., 1965], p. 15) in identifying Carl F. H. Henry as the one who broke through the decades of silence in 1947 with *The Uneasy Conscience of Modern Fundamentalism* (see Chap. 6). In his later writings Dr. Henry has frequently

pointed out that in expounding Biblical principles of social justice, and in openly challenging race discrimination and civil rights compromises, the evangelical task force ought to have been in the vanguard. Cf. *Aspects of Christian Social Action,* by Carl F. H. Henry (Grand Rapids, Mich.: Eerdmans Publishing Co., 1964), pp. 122-23.

9. 1 Peter 4:17.

10. The National Association of Evangelicals (NAE), through its headquarters in Wheaton, Ill.; its magazine, *United Evangelical Action;* its office of public affairs in Washington, D. C., and its chapters throughout the United States, is carrying on an increasingly active and useful program of participation in social affairs and interpretation of social problems.

11. Romans 12:17-18 (Phillips); Galatians 6:10 (Phillips); Philippians 4:5 (Phillips); 1 Thessalonians 3:12 (Phillips); 1 Thessalonians 5:14-15 (Phillips); 2 Timothy 2:24 (Phillips); Hebrews 12:14 (Phillips); 1 Peter 2:17 (RSV); Ephesians 2:10 (RSV); Titus 3:8 (RSV).

12. James 2:18.

13. Matthew 7:21-22.

Selected Bibliography

The books listed below include the works that were actively consulted in the writing of the present volume. Other references will be found in the notes. Still others, frequently used but of a more general nature, are unlisted. Some readers will note with dismay how few evangelical texts are mentioned. The lack is due to the dearth of writing in the field of social responsibility. A few evangelical authors whose works proved particularly helpful are marked with an asterisk (*).

BENNETT, JOHN C., ed. *Christian Social Ethics in a Changing World.* New York: Association Press, 1966.

BERDYAEV, NICOLAS. *The Destiny of Man.* Translated by Natalie Duddington. New York: Harper & Row; London: Geoffrey Bles, 1937.

BRACE, C. LORING. *Gesta Christi: A History of Humane Progress Under Christianity.* London: Hodder & Stoughton, 1884.

BREADY, J. WESLEY. *England: Before and After Wesley.* London: Hodder & Stoughton, 1938.

BRUNNER, EMIL. *The Divine Imperative.* Translated by Olive Wyon. London: Lutterworth Press, 1949.

BULL, GEOFFREY T. *When Iron Gates Yield.* Chicago: Moody Press, 1954.

BUTTERFIELD, HERBERT. *Christianity and History.* London: G. Bell & Sons, 1949; New York: Charles Scribner's Sons, 1950.

CHARTER, S. P. R. *Man on Earth.* Sausalito, Calif.: Contact Editions, Angel Island Publications, 1962.

DOBBIE, WILLIAM. *A Very Present Help.* Grand Rapids, Mich.: Zondervan Publishing Co., 1945.

EVANS, STANLEY G. *The Social Hope of the Church.* London: Hodder & Stoughton, 1965.

FAGLEY, RICHARD L. *The Population Explosion and Christian Responsibility.* New York: Oxford University Press, 1960.

FLETCHER, JOSEPH. *Situation Ethics*. Philadelphia: Westminster Press; London: SCM Press, 1966.

*FORD, LEIGHTON. *The Christian Persuader*. New York: Harper & Row, 1966.

FORRESTER, W. R. *Christian Vocation*. London: Lutterworth Press, 1945.

*GRAHAM, BILLY. *World Aflame*. Garden City, N. Y.: Doubleday & Co., 1966.

GRAY, ALEXANDER. *The Socialist Tradition*. London: Longmans, Green & Co., 1947.

*HEASMAN, KATHLEEN. *Evangelicals in Action*. London: Geoffrey Bles, 1962.

———. *Christians and Social Work*. London: SCM Press, 1965.

*HENRY, CARL F. H. *The Uneasy Conscience of Modern Fundamentalism*. Grand Rapids, Mich.: Eerdmans Publishing Co., 1947.

———. *Christian Personal Ethics*. Grand Rapids, Mich.: Eerdmans Publishing Co., 1957.

———. *Aspects of Christian Social Ethics*. Grand Rapids, Mich.: Eerdmans Publishing Co., 1964.

———. *Evangelicals at the Brink of Crisis*. Waco, Texas: Word Books, 1967.

HENRY, CARL F. H., and MOONEYHAM, W. STANLEY, eds. *One Race, One Gospel, One Task*. 2 vols. (Berlin: World Congress on Evangelism Reports, 1966.) Minneapolis, Minn.: World Wide Publications, 1967.

HOGBEN, ROWLAND. *Vocation*. London: Inter-Varsity Press, 1949.

*JONES, HOWARD O. *Shall We Overcome?* Westwood, N. J.: Fleming H. Revell, 1966.

*LINDSELL, HAROLD, ed. *The Church's Worldwide Mission*. Waco, Texas: Word Books, 1966.

———, ed. *Harper Study Bible*. New York: Harper & Row, 1964 (by permission of Zondervan Publishing Co., Grand Rapids, Michigan).

LUNN, ARNOLD, and LEAN, GARTH. *The New Morality*. London: Blandford Press, 1964.

———. *The Cult of Softness*. London: Blandford Press, 1965.

McCONNELL, FRANCIS T. *Evangelicals, Revolutionists and Idealists.* Nashville, Tenn.: Abingdon Press, 1942.

MILLER, ALEXANDER. *The Christian Significance of Karl Marx.* London: SCM Press, 1946.

MILLER, ROBERT M. *American Protestantism and Social Issues, 1919-1939.* Asheville, N. C.: University of North Carolina Press, 1958.

*MOBERG, DAVID O. *Inasmuch: Christian Social Responsibility in the Twentieth Century.* Grand Rapids, Mich.: Eerdmans Publishing Co., 1965.

NEWTON, JOHN (1725-1807). *Thoughts upon the African Slave Trade* (c. 1780), in *Works,* R. CECIL, ed. 6 vols. London, 1808.

NIEBUHR, REINHOLD. *Moral Man and Immoral Society.* New York: Charles Scribner's Sons, 1932.

*ORR, J. EDWIN. *The Second Evangelical Awakening in Britain.* London: Marshall, Morgan & Scott, 1949.

————. *The Light of the Nations.* Grand Rapids, Mich.: Eerdmans Publishing Co., 1965.

ROGERS, EDWARD. *Poverty on a Small Planet.* New York: The Macmillan Co., 1965.

*SMITH, TIMOTHY. *Revivalism and Social Reform.* Nashville, Tenn.: Abingdon Press, 1957.

TEMPLE, WILLIAM. *Christianity and Social Order.* London: Penguin Books, 1942.

————. *Nature, Man and God.* London: Macmillan & Co., 1949.

TROELTSCH, ERNST. *The Social Teaching of the Christian Churches.* Translated by Olive Wyon. 2 vols. New York: The Macmillan Co.; London: Allen & Unwin, 1931.

* TRUEBLOOD, D. ELTON. *Foundations for Reconstruction.* New York: Harper & Brothers, 1946.

————. *Your Other Vocation.* New York: Harper & Row, 1952.

WEBER, MAX. *The Protestant Ethic and the Spirit of Capitalism.* Translated by Talcott Parsons. London: Allen & Unwin, 1948.

WESTIN, GUNNAR. *The Free Church Through the Ages.* Translated by Virgil A. Olson. Nashville, Tenn.: Broadman Press, 1958.

WHITE, BOUCK. *The Call of the Carpenter*. Garden City, N. Y.:
Doubleday, Page & Co., 1914.

WILLIAMS, CHARLES. *The Descent of the Dove*. New York: Pellegrini & Cudahy, 1939.

Index

Abdullah the Mohammedan, 166
Abortion, 140-42
Abraham, 13, 56
Acton, Lord (John Emerich Edward Dalberg), 71
Adams, President John, 70
Alcohol, 52, 94, 144-45
Alfred the Great, 118
Amos, 8, 43-44, 76
Anabaptists, 16, 92
Ananias, 4
Appeasement, 120-21
Aristides, Marcianus, 29-30
Arnold of Brescia, 31
Augustine, 7
Automation, 52, 60, 106

Barabbas, 9
Barnes, Harry Elmer, 147
Barth, Karl, 25-26, 158
Beecher, Edward, 147, 160, 166
Bennett, John C., 165
Berdyaev, Nicolas, 100-101, 124, 164
Bérenger of Tours, 31
Birth control, 52, 110; see also population explosion
Black Muslims, 4
Blumhardt, Christoph, 49, 148, 160
Bond, James Emory, 89-90
Bonhoeffer, Dietrich, 21, 158
Boulding, Kenneth, 60
Bowie, Walter Russell, 158

Brace, C. Loring, 159
Brethren of the Common Life, 31
Brotherhood of Man, 4
Brunner, Emil, 4, 61-62
Bunyan, John, 1
Butterfield, Herbert, 18, 36, 159

Call, calling, 55-57, 61-63; see also vocation
Calvin, John, 47, 72-73, 124
Calvinism, 39, 71-72
Campbell, Arch, 165
Campbell, Douglas, 71
Capital punishment, 138-40
Carey, William, 33
Chalmers, James, 33
Chamberlain, Nathan H., 162
Chamberlain, Neville, 114
Charter, S. P. R., 107, 164
Chaucer, Geoffrey, 55
Child labor, 36, 42
Child stealing, 33
Christian Century, 98, 119, 164
Christian Medical Society, 141, 166
Christianity Today, 47, 165
Chrysostom, John, 7
Church, churches, 3-4, 9, 11, 16, 18, 47, 65, 129, 149-51, 165; historic social attitudes, 27-36; social pronouncements, 133-34; and abortion, 140-41; and alcohol, 144-145; and capital punishment, 138-140; and

democracy, 69-78; and euthanasia, 141-42; and highway safety, 136-37; and labor, 59-63; and morality, 91-101; and poverty, 134-36; and race, 79-90; and sex, 91-101, 142-44; and social gospel, 39-46; and the state, 16, 73, 127, 130-34; and stewardship of the earth, 103-12; and tobacco, 146; and war, 113-28
Churchill, Sir Winston, 118
Civil rights, 52, 82, 89, 100, 167
Clapham sect, 36
Coe, George A., 147
Coillard, François, 33
Communism, Communists, 43, 51, 77, 93, 118-24, 132-33
Congress on the Church's World-wide Mission, 150, 160
Conservatism, 2, 20, 43, 53, 69, 142
Constantine the Great, 31
Cromwell, Oliver, 72

Darrow, Clarence, 138
Darwin, Charles, 44-45, 96
David, King, 26, 99, 143
De Man, Henri, 38
Discrimination, 9, 12, 69
Divorce, 24
Dobbie, Gen. Sir William, 165
Donatus the Great, 31
Drug addiction, 94, 146
Duff, Alexander, 33
Durkheim, Emile, 45

Eckhart, Meister, 31
Ecumenicity, 6-8, 133
Eliot, John, 34
Eliot, Sir John, 74
Elizabeth I, Queen, 73, 77
Eshleman, Byron, 166
Ethics, 11, 16, 48, 52-53, 69-70, 98, 101, 130; of Jesus, 23; existential, 96-97; medical, 140; naturalistic, 96-97; relativistic, 94-97; situation, 95, 97-100; social, 53, 95, 97, 100; theological, 96; utilitarian, 94, 97; vocational, 62
Euthanasia, 141-42

Evangelical revival, 39, 48, 76
Evangelical undertow, 2
Evangelicalism, viii, 3, 20, 34, 43, 48, 150
Evangelism, 50, 58, 129, 132, 152, 154
Evans, Stanley G., 11-12, 112, 157, 164
Ezekiel, 9

Federal Council of Churches (now National Council), 41-43, 133
Fellowship of Christian Athletes, 92-93
Fenton, Horace L., Jr., x, 150, 153, 166
Finney, Charles G., 39-40, 88
Fletcher, Joseph, 95
Fliedner, Theodore, 160
Ford, Leighton, vii-viii
Forrester, W. R., 161
Francis of Assisi, 7
Francke, August, 160
Freud, Sigmund, 45-46, 96, 143
Friends of God, 31
Fundamentalism, 20, 47-48

Gaebelein, Frank E., ix, 165
Gairdner, Temple, 33
Garrison, William Lloyd, 40
Geneva Bible, 73, 77
Gibbon, Edward, 16
Gilmour, James, 33
Gladden, Washington, 160
Good Samaritan, parable of, 23
Graham, Billy, xi, 2, 80, 135, 154

Hampden, John, 74
Hardie, James Keir, 49, 60
Harris, Helen H., 158
Hawthorne experiments, 38, 63
Henry, Carl F. H., x, 2, 47-48, 166-67
Herod Antipas, 16, 24
Herod the Great, 13
Highway safety, 136-37, 140
Himmelfarb, Gertrude, 160
Hitler, Adolf, 114, 117
Holmes, Justice Oliver Wendell, 95, 163

Holy Spirit, 3-4, 8, 15, 20, 22, 28-29, 50, 53, 57, 66-67, 75, 83, 90, 92, 123, 128, 129, 132-33, 142, 149, 151
Homosexuality, 52-53, 100, 142-44
Homrighausen, Elmer G., 93, 98
Hooker, Richard, 162
Hooker, Thomas, 74-75
Hoover, President Herbert, 114
Hopkins, C. H, 159
Hosea, 8-9
Hunger, 60, 134-36; see also poverty
Hus, John, 27
Hutchinson, Anne, 74
Huxley, Aldous, 148
Huxley, Thomas, 45
Hyams, Edward, 112

Individualism, 70, 75-77
Inquisition, 31, 111
Intermarriage, 87, 163
Isaiah, 6, 8-19, 44, 66, 88, 104, 108
Israel, ancient, 8-10, 13, 25, 49-50, 69, 143; modern, 13, 121, 135

James, the Lord's brother, 6-8, 14-15, 44, 50, 67, 114, 154
Jefferson, President Thomas, 68, 130
Jeremiah, 8-9
Jesus Christ, need for commitment to, viii, xi, 1, 3, 6-7, 16, 28, 43, 55, 60-61, 63, 70, 75-79, 83-85, 88-89, 92, 106, 111, 115, 124, 129-32, 134, 139, 144, 146, 148-53, 155, 165; referred to as Lord, viii, 5-6, 9, 16, 19, 21-22, 24-28, 32, 41, 43, 54-55, 57, 63-64, 66, 80, 101, 111-13, 115, 116, 123, 125, 129, 132, 136, 143-45, 148-51, 153; social views of, 5, 8-9, 13, 18-26, 37, 39, 41, 44, 46-47, 50-53, 59-60, 63, 66-67, 80-81, 99-101, 105, 108, 114-15, 128, 136, 149-51, 154, 158
Jews, 117; see also Israel
John the Apostle, 83
John the Baptist, 8, 14, 16, 23
Jonah, 56
Jones, Sam, evangelist, 44
Josephus, Flavius, 157

Judson, Adoniram, 33
Justinian, Emperor, 31

Kant, Immanuel, 96, 163
Kellogg-Briand Peace Pact, 114-15, 117
Kingdom of God, 18, 23-25, 143, 150
Kinsey, Alfred C., 93, 163
Kipling, Rudyard, 124, 165
Klein, Justice Arthur G., 95, 163
Knapp, Jacob, 40

Labor, organized, 59-60
Last Judgment, parable of, 24, 84
Laubach, Frank C., 2
Law, Mosaic, 10, 139, 143
Law, Roman, 17, 132
Lawrence, D. H., 161
Le Play, Frédéric, 37-38
Leavitt, Joshua, 40
Lenin, V. I., 111, 158
Letter to Diognetus, 30
Lewis, C. S., 71-72, 162
Lincoln, President Abraham, 118
Livingstone, David, 33
Love, as Christian motivation, 53, 82-84, 99; as ethical practice, 95, 98-99, 101
Lowell, James Russell, 97, 163
Luke the evangelist, 15
Lung cancer, 146
Luther, Martin, 27, 34, 61, 112, 124
Lyall, Leslie, 157

MacArthur, Gen. Douglas, 118
Mackay, John A., 37, 91
MacLeod, George Lord, 60, 76
Madison, President James, 70, 115, 162
Magnificat, 12, 15
Malthus, Thomas R., 108-10
Mannes, Marya, 106, 164
Martyn, Henry, 33
Marx, Karl, 26, 45, 93
Marxism, Marxists, 4, 17, 43, 54, 58, 117, 119-20, 123-24, 131
Mary, Mother of Jesus Christ, 8, 13-15, 23
Mary Tudor, Queen, 73

Masefield, John, 4, 37, 157
May, Rollo, 160
McConnell, Francis T., 165
McLuhan, Marshall, 63, 100, 163
Mehl, Roger, 131
Mennonites, 16, 119
Messiah, 13-14, 22, 24, 30
Micah, 8-9
Mill, John Stuart, 71, 118, 162, 164
Millay, Edna St. Vincent, 129, 165
Miller, Alexander, 158
Milton, John, 47
Moberg, David O., 166
Moffat, Robert, 33
Morality, 99-101; see ethics, sexual morality
Morison, Samuel Eliot, 159
Morrison, Robert, 33
Moses, 8, 56, 163
Mumford, Lewis, 37, 159

National Association of Evangelicals, 167
National Council of Churches, 43
Negro, see race
Nelson, Senator Gaylord, 105, 108, 164
Neutrality, 119
New Morality, 93, 97
Newton, John, 35
Nichols, James Hastings, 2
Niebuhr, Reinhold, 162
Nommensen, Ludwig Ingwer, 33

Oberlin, Jean Frédéric, 34-35
Origen, 124

Pacifism, 119, 123, 164
Paton, Alan, 104-5, 164
Paton, John G., 33
Paul the Apostle, 4-5, 7, 15, 32, 57, 67, 72, 75, 81, 83, 99, 112, 139, 142-144, 163
Pax Romana, 31, 117
Peabody, Stephen, 160
Peace, 82, 113-28
Peace Corps, 52

Perpetua, 7
Peter the Apostle, 63, 67
Pico della Mirandola, 147, 166
Plum, H. G., 65, 161
Pollution: air, 110-11; land, 108-10; water, 107-8
Polygamy, 33
Pope, Alexander, 96
Population explosion, 51, 105, 110, 135
Poverty, 9, 11, 15, 30, 32, 35, 40, 42, 44, 51, 76, 124, 134-36
Power structures, 131-32
Prodigal Son, parable of, 105
Prohibition, 145
Puritans, Puritanism, 50, 65, 69-74, 76, 92-93, 100
Pym, John, 74

Quakers, 86, 119

Race, color, 15, 51, 74, 79-90, 95, 126, 138, 167; racial prejudice, 38, 69, 83
Ratramnus of Corbie, 31
Rauschenbusch, Walter, 40-41, 160
Reformation, 5, 16, 32, 34, 56, 76, 92
Rembrandt Van Rijn, 7
Renan, Ernest, 15
Revolution, 9, 13, 122, 126-27
Rilliet, Jean, 159
Robinson, John A. T., 95, 158
Robinson, Norman H. G., 62, 99, 161, 163
Rogers, Edward, 165
Roman Catholic Church, 32, 35, 48, 72-73, 130, 141
Russell, Bertrand, 120
Ruysbroeck, John, 31

Sabbath, 25-26, 30, 37
Sartre, Jean-Paul, 96
Sayers, Dorothy L., 160
Schmucker, Samuel, 40
Schwartz, Christian Friedrich, 33
Second Advent, 112, 116, 136
Servetus, Miguel, 72
Service, Robert W., 102
Sewall, Judge Samuel, 79, 162
Sexual morality, 93-101, 142-44

Shaftesbury, Lord (Anthony Ashley Cooper), 36, 159
Shields, Joseph, 165
Shute, Nevil (Norway), 103, 105, 110
Simon de Montfort, 111
Sittler, Joseph, 163
Slaves, slavery, 10-11, 16-18, 23, 31, 33, 35-36, 39-40, 66, 69, 88-89, 117-118, 159; slave traffic, 15, 17, 35-36, 165
Slessor, Mary, 33
Smith, Timothy L., 39, 160
Social gospel, 39-43
Spartacus, 17
Spence, H. D. M., 12, 157
Spencer, Herbert, 45-46
Spener, Philipp, 160
Stalin, Josef, 93
Stylites, Simeon, 9
Sunday, Billy, 44, 89
Symons, W. G., 56

Tauler, Johannes, 31, 159
Taylor, Graham, 160
Temple, William, 62, 149, 161, 166
Theresa of Avila, 31
Thermonuclear energy, 52, 103, 111, 117
Thielicke, Helmut, 76
Tobacco, 146
Transport for Christ, 137, 165
Troeltsch, Ernst, 18, 22, 158
Trueblood, D. Elton, 70, 162

United Evangelical Action, 167
United Nations, 125

Unjust Steward, parable of, 105
Unnatural sex, 142-44

Varus, Publius Quintilius, 13
Veniaminov, Innokenti, 33
Viet Cong, 4, 53
Vietnam war, 82, 113, 119-23, 125, 127
Viteles, M. S., 37-38, 159
Vocation, 55-58, 60-64, 136; see also call
von Weltz, Justinian, 34

Walker, G. S. M., 31, 159
Wang Ming-tao, 157
War, 9, 12, 31, 51, 82, 95, 114-16, 118-119, 121, 123-27, 132, 164
Warburton, William, 27, 158
Ward, Harry F., 160
Washington, Joseph R., Jr., 162
Weld, Theodore Dwight, 40
Wellhausen, Julius, 45-46
Wesley, John, 7, 35, 48, 159
Wheaton Declaration, 51-52
Wilberforce, William, 35-36, 159
Williams, Charles, 28, 158
Williams, John, 33
Witherspoon, John, 70
Women, 15, 23, 31, 42, 97
Work, conditions of, 36-39; as Christian vocation, 57-64
World Congress on Evangelism, 2
World Council of Churches, 3

Y.M.C.A., 48
Year of Jubilees, 10, 65-66

Zwingli, Ulrich, 7, 32, 47, 166